COLONIES OF HEAVEN

CELTIC
CHRISTIAN
COMMUNITIES

COLONIES OF HEAVEN

CELTIC

CHRISTIAN

COMMUNITIES

LIVE THE

TRADITION

IAN BRADLEY

Northstone

Cover design: Barbara Houston and Margaret Kyle

Celtic Christianity: Live the Tradition was published simultaneously in the United Kingdom as *Colonies of Heaven: Celtic Models for Today's Church* by Darton, Longman, and Todd, London, England.

Northstone Publishing acknowledges the financial support of the Government of Canada, through the Book Publishing Industry Development Program, for its publishing activities.

Northstone Publishing is an imprint of Wood Lake Books Inc., an employee-owned company, and is committed to caring for the environment and all creation. Northstone recycles, reuses, and composts, and encourages readers to do the same. Resources are printed on recycled paper and more environmentally friendly groundwood papers (newsprint), whenever possible. The trees used are replaced through donations to the Scoutrees for Canada program. A percentage of all profit is donated to charitable organizations.

Canadian Cataloguing in Publication Data
Bradley, Ian, 1950-
Celtic Christian communities
Running title: Colonies of heaven.
ISBN 1-896836-43-7
1. Celtic Church. I. Title. II. Title: Colonies of heaven.
BF748.B72 2000   274.1'0089'916   C00-910871-8

Published by Northstone Publishing
an imprint of Wood Lake Books Inc., Kelowna, BC Canada

Printing 10 9 8 7 6 5 4 3 2 1

Printed in Great Britain

Contents

Preface

This is my fourth book on the subject of Celtic
Christianity. My first, *The Celtic Way*, originally
published by Darton, Longman and Todd in 1993,
and now in its sixth reprinting having sold over
twelve thousand copies, was born of my discovery of
a neglected aspect of our Christian heritage which
seemed to speak with almost uncanny relevance to
many of the concerns of our present age. With
hindsight I can now see that it had rather too much
of the over-romantic and uncritical enthusiasm of the
new convert. My second book, *Columba, Pilgrim and
Penitent*, commissioned by the Iona Community for
the 1400th anniversary of Columba's death and
published by Wild Goose Publications in 1996,
presented a more sober study of major themes in
early Irish Christianity and their message for the
Church today. My third excursion into this field, *Celtic
Christianity: Making Myths and Chasing Dreams*, published

by Edinburgh University Press in 1999, can perhaps be best seen as an act of penitence on the part of someone who realised that his work had helped to fuel the current mood of Celto-mania and who was conscious of the need for a critical academic study of the whole phenomenon of Celtic Christian revivalism.

This last book might seem to have taken me firmly into the camp of the academic sceptics and demythologisers who, I had warned in my earlier studies, would destroy the essence of Celtic Christianity by bringing a coldly rationalistic and analytical approach to something that was essentially of the spirit and was not, in George MacLeod's memorable phrase, 'a fit subject for the analyst's table'.[1] It begins with the observation that

> in the context of the current revival, it is tempting to suggest that Celtic Christianity is less an actual phenomenon defined in historical and geographical terms than an artificial construct created out of wishful thinking, romantic nostalgia and the projection of all kinds of dreams about what should and might be.[2]

However, loyal readers will have noticed that for all my reductionist demythologising, I also stated in the introduction that 'I still believe that the distinctive voice of the early indigenous Christian communities of the British Isles speaks to us through all the layers of distortion and fabrication with which it has been overlaid'.[3]

This new book tries to listen to that distinctive voice and to discern its message for those of us seeking to live out the Christian faith in the post-modern culture of the twenty-first century. It is a book about contemporary models of being church which are suggested by the outlook and practices of the indigenous Christian communities of the British Isles between the sixth and eleventh centuries, the 'golden age' of so-called Celtic Christianity. I am much more conscious than when I began studying, teaching and writing about this subject nearly ten years ago just how little we really know about this period. I am also much more conscious that what we have come, for better or worse, to call 'Celtic Christianity' was not radically different from other early medieval inculturations of Christianity, be they Anglo-Saxon, Roman, Continental or Eastern Orthodox.

With these important provisos, however, I still think that it is possible to identify certain themes in the early Christian life of Britain and Ireland which, if certainly not unique, were distinctive and which are well worth our while looking at today. This is not a plea for a restorationist movement. I am emphatically not arguing for a new Celtic Church which seeks to re-create and replicate the forms and orders used by Columba, Patrick, David, Aidan and their successors. Rather I want to highlight certain themes which seem to me to be worth reconsidering and perhaps taking up again in different ways today. Several of them are indeed already being explored and put into practice. Whether they are 'Celtic' or not (whatever that means) ultimately does not matter. What does matter is whether they work, whether they speak to people today as authentic, honest and helpful, and above all whether they help to advance the Kingdom of God and to make us walk in closer imitation of Christ.

The title that I have chosen for this book epitomises both the problems and the possibilities implicit in this kind of enterprise. I cannot now recall where I first came across the phrase 'colonies of heaven' confidently quoted as a term that Columba and his contemporaries used to describe their monastic communities. Sad to say, I have not been able to find it in a single early source and I suspect that like other rather appealing phrases we attribute to our ancient Celtic Christian forebears, it is almost certainly apocryphal and only goes back to one of the relatively recent Celtic Christian revivals. The use of the term 'Wild Goose' to describe the Holy Spirit is a case in point – extensive research by myself and others has not been able to trace it back any further than the fertile imagination of George MacLeod. Yet in a sense it does not matter where the phrase 'colonies of heaven' comes from. The idea that it conveys, of the thin dividing line between the physical and the spiritual and the need to establish on earth places which speak of heaven, was certainly fundamental to Christian faith and practice in the British Isles in the so-called Dark Ages. It is most definitely a vision that we need to recapture if Christianity is to shine again in our own perhaps even darker age.

Each of the six chapters in this book follows the same format. The first half explores a particular theme as it was expressed and worked out in what for better or worse has come to be known as Celtic Christianity, both in its golden age from the sixth to the tenth centuries and in its later manifestations. The second half discusses the relevance of this theme today and suggests how it might be applied in practical terms to contemporary Christian life.

At various stages of their gestation the chapters which make up this book have been delivered as lectures at a conference on Celtic models for the Church led by Ray Simpson on Lindisfarne in October 1998, at an afternoon meeting of the Angus Theological Club organised by Harry Gibson in Dundee in February 1999, to pilgrims exploring Celtic spirituality in Scotland under the direction of Cintra Pemberton in September 1999, at an ecumenical evening at St John's Church, Pittenweem convened by Julian Randall in October 1999, at a Celtic Day at the Community of the Resurrection, Mirfield, West Yorkshire, set up by Brother William Nicol in November 1999, and at seminars of my Celtic Christianity honours class in the Divinity

School of St Andrews University during the 1999 Martinmas Semester. To all at those gatherings who responded both positively and negatively to what I had to say and who contributed new insights and suggestions, I am profoundly grateful. I particularly wish to thank Peter Millar and Julie McGuinness for allowing me to print their poems, Donald Allchin for letting me quote from his translations of Welsh poems, and Thomas Clancy and Gilbert Markus for permission to quote verses from their translation of Columba's *Altus Prosator*. The extract from T. S. Eliot's *Four Quartets* is reproduced by permission of Messrs Faber & Faber, the extract from Edith Sitwell's poem 'Praise We Great Men' from *The Outcasts* by permission of David Higham Associates, and George MacLeod's prayer 'A Veil Thin as Gossamer' by permission of Wild Goose Publications.

1

Colonies of Heaven – the Monastic Model

For those revisiting it nowadays either through exploring its sites or reading accounts of the lives of its leading exponents, perhaps the most striking feature of Celtic Christianity is its monastic character. The places particularly associated with this phase of the Christian history of the British Isles, and now meccas for tourists as well as for pilgrims – Iona, Glendalough, Clonmacnoise, Lindisfarne, St David's and Whithorn – are all primarily monastic sites. The classic texts of early Irish, Welsh and British spirituality, Adamnan's *Life of Columba*, Bede's *Life of Cuthbert*, the early lives of Samson, Gildas and David, the hermit poems, penitentials and prayers, were all written in monasteries and have monastic life and discipline as their main subject matter.

For Christians living in the British Isles between the fifth and eleventh centuries, the monastery rather than the parish church was the primary focus for worship, pastoral care and religious instruction. The key figures of authority in the Church tended to be abbots, running their often extensive *familia* or *parochiae* of monasteries, rather than bishops, who had a largely sacerdotal and liturgical role and did not have diocesan territorial responsibilities. Virtually all the indigenous 'saints' whose lives and legends dominate the ecclesiastical history of the British Isles in this period were monks. The best-known of them, Ninian, Columba, David, Columbanus, Aidan and Cuthbert, were also founders of monasteries. It has recently been persuasively argued that Patrick, the one prominent Celtic saint who is not normally seen as a monk, almost certainly came from a monastic tradition and was deeply imbued with the monastic outlook.[1] His remark that the sons and daughters of Scotic chieftains became monks and virgins for Christ is often cited to show the pull of the monastic life in Ireland at the dawning of the 'golden age' of Celtic Christianity.

A word of caution should be entered here. Because virtually all of our sources for this period, both written and archaeological, tend to come from monasteries, there is a danger of overemphasising its monastic character. We know virtually nothing of the

Christian life that took place outside the monasteries, but that does not mean it did not exist or was insignificant. Over-romantic portrayals of monks imbued with a superhuman sanctity and asceticism may also have distorted our view of the golden age of Celtic Christianity. Many of the documents that describe monastic life in this period probably represent ideals rather than reality. The comment by Wendy Davies, the leading expert on early medieval Wales, that 'the popular view of the Celtic church assigns a power to monastic institutions which is difficult to support in Wales', has been echoed by recent scholars in respect of other parts of the British Isles.[2] It is now clear that later hagiography exaggerated both the number of monasteries and the role of well known early saints in their foundation. Nonetheless, even among revisionist historians there is a general consensus that the *monasterium* was the key ecclesiastical institution in the British Isles until the development of parish churches and territorial dioceses in the aftermath of the Norman conquest. Wendy Davies herself concedes that 'support for the fact, at least, of monasticism in early Wales is not hard to find' and that the evidence strongly suggests that churches were attached to religious communities rather than lay villages.[3] She has, indeed, computed that in south-east Wales alone at the time of the Norman conquest there were at least fifty monasteries, many of them very small, the great majority of which had probably been established in the late

[3]

sixth and early seventh centuries. Kathleen Hughes' extensive research suggests a similar burst of monastery-making in Ireland in the same period.[4] In Scotland the great era of monastic foundation came slightly later.

Recent scholarship has also made clear that there was nothing distinctively 'Celtic' about a church organised around monasteries rather than parishes. A very similar situation prevailed in the Anglo-Saxon church until the establishment of settled parishes in England in the eleventh and twelfth centuries. An important recent study, *Pastoral Care before the Parish*, has shown how flawed is the stereotypical view of an Irish (and therefore Celtic) church based on monastic *parochiae* and wandering monks contrasting with an Anglo-Saxon (and therefore English) church organised into territorial dioceses and with resident parish priests. In Anglo-Saxon England monasteries staffed by pastorally active religious communities gradually came to assume the role of mother churches, or minsters, and exercised control over lesser churches. In the words of Richard Sharpe, one of the book's editors, 'before the development of the parish it is now accepted that in England pastoral care was organized through large "parishes" served by teams of priests and other clergy operating from important central churches – these churches are familiarly called minsters, translation of *monasterium*.'[5]

The fact that the *monasterium*, in its role as minster, played a central role in the ecclesiastical life of Anglo-

Saxon England does not, of course, diminish its importance in the Celtic realms of Ireland, Scotland and Wales. What we can now say with some certainty, indeed, is that across the British Isles, in the seven centuries or so between the departure of the Romans and the arrival of the Normans, monasteries were the main providers of Christian worship, pastoral care and evangelism. When eventually they were supplanted by a network of parish churches grouped into territorial dioceses under the control of a bishop, the new episcopal sees were often established on the sites of old monastic communities, as at Durham, St David's, Dunkeld, St Andrews, Brechin, Armagh, Kells and Llandaff.

The strongly monastic character of the Church in this period affected the nature of its ministry and witness in a number of ways. First, it produced a model of ministry that was collegiate and communitarian rather than individualistic. Commenting on the situation of clergy in early medieval Wales, Wendy Davies notes that 'community life seems to have been the norm, whether or not the community was composed of professed monks, for we hear nothing of the isolated cleric'.[6] Ministry in all its aspects, liturgical, pastoral, evangelistic, educational, was not the solitary individualistic task it so often is today. It was rather undertaken by teams of men and women, ordained and lay, who lived together in community and operated from a common central base from which they went out among the people preaching, teaching, baptising, administering the sacraments, caring for the sick and burying the dead. Community life in some form was the normal and accepted expression of vocation, not just to monastic profession but also to clerical orders of any kind and indeed to a variety of lay ministries.

This brings us to the second striking feature of Celtic and Anglo-Saxon monasticism which is the great variety of types of ministry which it embraced and encompassed. The parochial pattern of church organisation, which supplanted it in the eleventh and twelfth centuries and which has been the dominant model ever since, has tended to focus on just one kind of ministry, that of the full-time parish minister or priest, mostly on his own (and for the great majority of the time ministry has been an all-male preserve). As used in the British Isles in the centuries between the departure of the Romans and the coming of the Normans, the word *monasterium* covered a huge range of different communities, from tiny settlements of two or three hermits' huts to townships comprising several thousand people. Monasteries could be made up entirely of hermits or anchorites, of those living a cenobitic or communal life or of a mixture of both solitaries and monks living in community. They could be single-sex institutions or communities of both sexes, some of whose members led celibate lives and others of whom were married. Some monastic communities had just one priest attached to them and were largely made up of non-ordained monks, others had no members under monastic vows and were essentially teams of regular clergy undertaking a largely pastoral role in the surrounding area. Within some of the larger monasteries, solitary hermits lived and prayed alongside married monks; professed monks and nuns coexisted with lay brothers and sisters; regular and secular clergy, ordained and non-ordained, men and women, shared their common life with the many pilgrims, penitents and other guests who regularly stayed in the *hospitium*.

Alongside its communal aspect, this variety of types of ministry and Christian witness was perhaps the most significant consequence of the predominantly monastic hue of the Celtic and Anglo-Saxon churches. As the medieval historian Alan Thacker observes,

> It is now abundantly clear that the term *monasterium* and its English equivalent, 'minster', embraced communities of very different size and status, with very different ways of life. Undoubtedly some, such as Bede's Jarrow, were close to the strict Benedictine ideal. They, however, were the exception. Many others seem to have been loosely organized establishments ruled by an abbot and housing priests and other inmates who might be described as *monachi* or *clerici*.[7]

Celtic and Anglo-Saxon monasteries varied in func-

[7]

tion as well as in size and composition. Some existed primarily as retreats and houses of prayer, others as bases for missionary work and pastoral care.

A third striking feature of churches based on a monastic rather than a parochial model of organisation was their high level of commitment and discipline. Monasteries are places where people go willingly to live under rules and authority. They are communities of intention, made up of those who have taken certain vows and accepted a certain lifestyle. Celtic and Anglo-Saxon *monasteria* included people with widely differing levels of commitment. Not all were wedded to vows of poverty, chastity and obedience (and, unlike those entering Benedictine monasteries on the Continent of Europe, none made vows of stability binding them to remain for ever in the house where they made their first profession). It is reasonable to assume, however, and the carefully graded lists of punishments for different categories of offender prescribed in the Irish penitentials confirm this, that all those living within the bounds of the monastic ditch, or *vallum*, lived according to some kind of disciplinary code and accepted the authority of the abbot.

In many ways, indeed, Celtic and Anglo-Saxon monasteries were highly authoritarian communities. This aspect tends to be rather glossed over, if not ignored, by many modern enthusiasts for Celtic Christianity. Much is made of the family nature of the monasteries. It is certainly true that they were often grouped together into a monastic *familia* and that the Irish word for family, *muintir*, derives from *monasterium*. If we want to make this analogy, however, it is of the hierarchical and patriarchal (or matriarchal) Victorian family that we should be thinking rather than some kind of 1960s-style hippy commune where everyone is allowed to do their own thing and all you need is love. Irish monasteries in particular were run on very strict lines by their abbots who exercised all the discipline and exuded all the *gravitas* of the most severe Victorian *paterfamilias*. The institutions over which they presided were not egalitarian communities. There were clearly established hierarchies and the professed monks constituted an élite of crack combat troops or *milites Christi*, doing battle with the devil and supported by a multitude of camp-followers whose role was essentially supportive.

In part this élitism sprang from a recognition that people have different gifts and are called to different kinds of ministry, some more demanding and radical in their commitment than others. It also reflected the norms and values of a highly stratified society. It is significant that Patrick writes particularly of the sons and daughters of Irish chieftains becoming monks and nuns, and that so many of the leading Celtic saints and monastic founders are portrayed as being of noble family, Columba being perhaps the best-known example. It is clear that the monasteries did attract a number of high-born recruits and that it was these figures who tended to rise to the top and become abbots and abbesses. There were very close connections between monastic foundations and the ruling dynasties of Celtic and Anglo-Saxon kingdoms. The rule of an abbot, who was often known as *princeps*, over his monastic *familia* had many similarities to that of a king over his *tuath*. Certainly it became common for abbacies to be held by certain families and to be passed down in a form of hereditary succession.

It is often said that monasteries flourished in Irish society because they suited its tribal nature. Many monasteries, perhaps indeed the majority, were royal foundations, established through grants of land and endowments by kings motivated by a desire to consolidate and legitimate their power and gain the backing of the Church, as well as by more pious intentions and genuine religious convictions. In return for this support and endowment, monasteries supported the secular rulers, providing them with coronation services to give them spiritual as well as temporal authority, and supplying pastoral care and the ordinances of religion to their subjects. Unlike parish churches, they were charged with pastoral responsibility not so much for a territorial area as for a community defined according to ties of kinship, family and loyalty to a particular ruler. To that extent, the ministry of the monastery was tribal rather than universal, although the principle of hospitality meant that no one was turned away if they came in search of help or sanctuary of any kind.

In many respects Celtic monastic life was based on the monasticism which flourished in Egypt and Palestine in the fourth and fifth centuries. The desert fathers pioneered both the eremitic (solitary) and cenobitic (communal) strands of monasticism which so often existed side by side in Irish communities. There was, however, one key difference between the two traditions. Whereas the monks in the desert communities generally sought and practised radical separation from the world, many of the monasteries in the British Isles were intensely involved in the affairs of the world and the lives of the people they served as well as being places of withdrawal and sanctuary. In scattered rural communities with virtually no other institutions or centres, they fulfilled the roles of hospital, hotel, school, university, arts workshop, open prison and reformatory, night shelter and drop-in day centre as well as church, retreat house, mission station and place of prayer and spiritual healing. They concerned themselves not just with the spiritual, intellectual and physical well-being of the tribal communities which they served but also with their culture and tradition. As well as copying the Psalms and Gospels, those working in the monastic scriptoria wrote down for posterity the stories, poems and songs of pre-Christian Celtic culture. The monasteries took on the role of being keepers and preservers of traditional myths and legends. Unlike later Continental foundations, many were places of intense coming and going, not cut off from the outside world and hidden behind high walls, but open and accessible to a constant stream of visitors, pilgrims and penitents.

One of the most costly and demanding tasks undertaken by the monasteries in early medieval Ireland, Scotland, England and Wales was the exercise of a constant ministry of hospitality. Often the guest-house, or *hospitium*, was given the choicest site within the monastic settlement and its residents were regularly given the best food and drink. The lives of both Celtic and Anglo-Saxon saints are filled with stories illustrating their concern to make visitors welcome. Columba supposedly wrote two of the hymns which are commonly attributed to him while grinding oats to make bread for guests expected on Iona. The monastery which he founded at Derry is said to have provided meals for a thousand hungry people each day. The early Irish life of Brigid speaks of her continually breaking bread and making butter for those visiting the mixed monastery over which she presided at Kildare. Tradition has it that when churning butter she always made thirteen portions – twelve in honour of the apostles and an extra one in honour of Christ, which was reserved for guests and the poor. The monks at David's monastery in Pembrokeshire fed off bread and water but cooked sumptuous meals for their guests. Bede tells of how Cuthbert, serving as guest-master of a new monastery at Ripon in the depths of winter, found a young man sitting in the guest-house. He 'got water to wash his hands, washed his feet himself, dried them, put them in his bosom and humbly chafed them with his hands'.[8] Later Cuthbert cooked a meal for the youth only to find that he had gone, although there were no footprints in the snow. Returning to the kitchen he found three newly and apparently miraculously baked loaves lying on the table. He was convinced that God had sent an angel to encourage the ministry of hospitality in the newly founded monastery.

The sense that in hosting strangers, they might well be entertaining angels, or even Christ himself, extended to the Celtic saints' dealings with non-human visitors. Columba taught the monks on Iona to show hospitality to the birds which came to the island. Once, according to Adamnan, he called one of the brothers and told him to watch out for a crane flying over from Ireland. When it arrived, the bird was to be carried up from the shore, taken to the monastery and fed and looked after for three days. The crane duly flew in and the brother did as he had been bidden. Columba commended him: 'God bless you, my son, because you have tended well our pilgrim guest.'[9] Another story recounts how Kevin of Glendalough was once engaged in the cross vigil with his arms outstretched when a blackbird came and laid a clutch of eggs in the palm of his hands. Not wishing to disturb the bird, the saint maintained his vigil until the baby birds had hatched.

As well as having their physical needs cared for,

visitors to the monasteries were also given pastoral care and spiritual counselling. The cure of souls was one of the primary functions of both the Celtic monastic communities and the Anglo-Saxon minsters. Indeed, several scholars have recently suggested that many *monasteria* may have been established principally for the purpose of dispensing pastoral care. The great Celtic and Anglo-Saxon saints are often portrayed by their biographers performing pastoral roles. According to the eleventh-century *Life* by Rhygyfarch, David baptised, preached, prayed for the dead and looked after orphans, widows, the poor and the infirm as well as having a special care for pilgrims. Bede noted how people flocked to Lindisfarne to receive counselling and care from Aidan and expressly praised Hilda for ministering to those living outside the monastic community at Whitby – 'to her came the ordinary people, as well as kings and princes, for help and advice'.[10] Adamnan showed Columba exercising a predominantly pastoral ministry on Iona, guiding his monks and receiving, blessing and counselling visitors.

The hospitality and pastoral care practised in the Celtic and Anglo-Saxon monasteries was part and parcel of a broader ministry of presence and availability in which the Church's primary role was conceived of as simply being there in the midst of the people. This ministry of presence was exercised both inside and outside the confines of the monastic *vallum*. As well as patiently listening to and counselling the penitents who came to them, monks went out in twos and threes into the countryside to preach and provide pastoral support. Much of their work was probably done in the open air or in people's homes rather than in designated ecclesiastical buildings. John Blair and Richard Sharpe point out that in the centuries before the establishment of parish churches 'the primary aspects of pastoral care need not have depended on the existence of either structures or buildings'.[11] Open-air baptism may well have been the norm, and this perhaps explains why there are far fewer remains of fonts or separate baptismal churches in the great religious sites of Britain and Ireland from this period than in similar sites in Gaul or Italy.

The exercise of this pastoral ministry of presence was seen as a more important function for the Church than engaging in mission or evangelism. This is perhaps a rather difficult point to grasp in our age when every organisation seems to need its mission statement, every church its evangelism plan and every theological school its department of missiology. We have tended to view the motivations and actions of the Celtic saints as though they shared our modern priorities. A classic case is Columba, who is so often portrayed as the great apostle of Scotland and the man who converted the Picts to Christianity. In fact, it is highly doubtful if Columba ever saw himself as a missionary in the modern sense of that term and if he converted more than a handful of

Picts. He spent relatively little time travelling through mainland Scotland proselytising and preaching. He certainly saw himself as a witness to Christ, a *marturos* indeed, but his deep and radical discipleship was expressed in a life spent largely in prayer, study, listening and healing rather than in dashing around seeking heathens to convert.

Men and women entered monasteries in this period, as they have ever since, out of a strong sense of vocation and in order to learn how to live their lives in obedience to God. Above all else, the monasteries of early medieval Britain and Ireland were communities of prayer. At the heart of the *monasterium* was the church, in Celtic communities generally made of wood and in Anglo-Saxon ones of stone, in which the monks assembled together, usually five times during the day and three times during the night, to recite the Divine Office. This continual offering of praise, prayer and petition, chiefly through the chanting of the Psalms, was the focus of the monastic life. Communally in the chapel and individually in their cells, the monks fulfilled Paul's injunction in 1 Thessalonians 5.17 to 'pray without ceasing'.

Together with the prayer that formed the core of their lives, monks engaged in hard manual labour and study. Their daily regime, carefully prescribed in the rule associated with each foundation and often attributed to one of the leading saints, was tough and demanding. Discipline, obedience and commitment were central to monastic life. To be a monk was to be a martyr and specifically to practise white martyrdom, that form of Christian witness so dear to the Irish saints, which involved dying to self and to all attachments, leaving home and family and going into perpetual exile as a pilgrim for Christ. The rules for the Irish monasteries in particular have a severity not found in those associated with the Continental orders:

> Take not of food till thou art hungry. Sleep not till thou feelest desire. Speak not except on business. Thy measure of prayer shall be until thy tears come; or thy measure of work of labour till thy tears come; or thy measure of thy work of labour or of thy genuflections until thy perspiration often comes, if thy tears are not free.[12]

These strictures applied only to those under full monastic profession. Secular clergy and the various groups of lay men and women attached to monastic communities lived under rules which were less severe but still demanding. If life within Celtic and Anglo-Saxon monasteries was highly prescribed and disciplined, however, it was also balanced and rhythmic. The individual monk's day was structured to provide a balance between the spiritual, the physical and the intellectual. Over a longer timescale, there was a rhythm of engagement in and withdrawal from the world that is very different from the radical separation and escape to the desert of the Egyptian monastic tradition. Once again, this feature is well illustrated in the lives of some of the best-known Celtic and Anglo-Saxon saints. Columba alternated periods of intense activity, running his large and complex monastic *familia* from Iona and dabbling in the politics of his native Ireland, with months of solitude on the island of Hinba. Cuthbert withdrew periodically from the frantic business of running the community at Lindisfarne and treating with Northumbrian kings and princes to his hermit cell on the uninhabited Farne islands. In Wales, Dyfrig regularly retreated from the busy monastery at Llantwit Major to Caldy Island. Samson found even that island retreat too crowded and retired with three companions to a cave near the river Severn.

In other respects, too, the pattern of life in Celtic monasteries was characterised by a sense of balance and rhythm, between solitude and community, activity and contemplation, worship and pastoral care. This balance was broken in the later Middle Ages when there came to be a much sharper distinction between regular and secular clergy, contemplatives and active pastors. There was also a fine balance between the monastery's role as a community resource and as a sacred space. The *vallum* or ditch which surrounded the monastery was not designed as a barrier to the outside world but rather served to keep domestic animals in and wild beasts out. It also delineated an area that was to be regarded as sacred and in which the values of the Kingdom of God rather than of the world of humankind would prevail. Violence of any kind was legally and absolutely prohibited within the monastic enclosure, which was to be a place free from all aggression. As a result, Celtic monasteries were often used by people to place their valuables for safe keeping and gave sanctuary to those who were fleeing violence or who had themselves committed serious crimes, including murder.

Rooted in the world, serving it and intimately involved in its affairs, yet embodying radically otherworldly values, the Celtic monasteries were, indeed, 'colonies of heaven' planted on earth to point as a sign and harbinger of the Kingdom that was yet to come. Philip Sheldrake has written particularly perceptively of this view of the monastic enclosure as a 'privileged space within which a particular vision of the world could be lived out' in his book *Living Between Worlds*:

> Monks in the tradition of Columbanus saw
> monastic settlements as anticipations of para-
> dise in which the forces of division, violence
> and evil were excluded. Wild beasts were
> tamed and nature was regulated. The privileges
> of Adam and Eve in Eden, received from God
> but lost in the Fall, were reclaimed. The living
> out of this vision of an alternative world in-
> volved all the people who were brought within
> the enclosed space. It was not something that

concerned merely the 'professional' ascetics.
The Columbanian tradition, for example,
believed that all people were called from birth
to the experience of contemplation. So,
'monastic' enclosures were places of spiritual
experience and non-violence and also places of
education, wisdom and art. Within the enclosures there took place, ideally speaking, an
integration of all the elements of human life,
as well as of all classes of human society.[13]

Are there aspects of the *monasterium*, both as it was
conceived and as it functioned in the British Isles
between the sixth and eleventh centuries, that might
help churches today as they seek new ways of witness
to Christ in a predominantly secular society?

I start from the recognition that the model of
being church that has served us well for much of the
second millennium is now under severe strain and
no longer able to deliver an effective ministry or
Christian presence in many parts of the country. The
parish system introduced in the aftermath of the
Norman conquest, and based on the principle of
a single priest or minister serving the people of a
particular geographical area, was not seriously chal-
lenged by the Reformation and has continued to be
at the heart of the ministry not just of established

national churches like the Church of England and the Church of Scotland but also of the Roman Catholic Church, the disestablished Anglican churches in Wales, Scotland and Ireland and the main Nonconformist denominations like the Baptists, Methodists and United Reformed Church. It is now manifestly collapsing under a number of strains, the most severe being shortage of money and human resources. Vocations to full-time ordained ministry have declined dramatically in recent decades, catastrophically in the case of the Roman Catholic Church. Even if there were to be a sudden upsurge in the number of those coming forward for ordination, there is not enough money in any of the main denominations to pay their stipends. The last thirty years have already seen a radical departure from the old principle of every parish having its own full-time resident priest or minister. In all the mainstream churches parishes have been amalgamated, clergy numbers drastically reduced and buildings declared redundant. It is not uncommon now in rural areas for one clergyperson to be serving up to half a dozen congregations. The strains on the diminishing band of clergy, now more isolated than ever, are all too clear in the rising levels of ministerial burn-out, stress, broken marriages and resignations.

One of the key aspects of the *monasterium* model that we could do with recapturing today is its provision of a wide variety of different types of ministry operating from a communal base. Already in response to the shortage of full-time ordained clergy, lack of finance and, more positively, to a much greater commitment to lay participation and involvement of all the people of God, all sorts of new styles of part-time ministry are being developed. These include non-stipendiary priests and locally ordained ministers in the Church of England, auxiliary ministers in the Church of Scotland and lay eucharistic ministers in the Roman Catholic Church. Greater use is being made of readers and deacons. Although some small progress has been made towards the development of team ministries in some areas, the majority of these new types of ministry continue to function according to the individualistic model associated with traditional full-time clergy. Should we not be exploring the development of a new kind of *monasterium* which would provide a base and some kind of community for teams of ministers, ordained and lay, full- and part-time, male and female, recognised as having different gifts and being called to varied vocations?

It is unrealistic and probably unnecessary to suggest that we go the whole hog in imitation of the *monasterium* model and attempt to set up residential communities where ministerial teams live together. There is a growing trend towards living in community and maybe some such modern monasteries will evolve over the coming decades. A less radical but still effective way of fostering a sense of shared spirituality and commitment is through people regularly eating together. This has been well demonstrated through the important part that meals have played in the highly successful Alpha course programme. Regular meals shared by clerical and lay colleagues in ministerial teams could do much to build up a sense of common purpose and identity. They would not have to be taken in silence!

There are other ways of fostering the shared discipline and commitment to a way of life, as well as the communal and collegial atmosphere of the monastery, to create a greater sense of community among those involved in ministry. Existing institutions like deanery, diocesan or provincial synods, presbyteries or circuits could be encouraged to take on this role. Perhaps even more appropriate than these denominational structures as ready-made communities which could be developed to take on something of the ethos and function of the Celtic and Anglo-Saxon monastery are local inter-denominational networks such as ministers' fraternals and councils of churches. The *monasterium* model flourished at a time when there was no denominational agenda but rather a strong sense of one universal Church with its own strong local and regional identity. How marvellous if the new-style *monasteria* could be modelled on an ecumenical and non-denominational basis and become colonies of heaven in their anticipation of a post-denominational future when the unity of the body of Christ is once again actualised in his churches on earth.

At present clergy are almost unique among the so-called caring professions in having to work largely in almost total isolation from their colleagues. Nearly all doctors nowadays are members of group practices and work out of health centres which often also house nurses and other specialist staff. Social workers are grouped in teams and share offices with colleagues. Teachers, hard pressed as they are, have the camaraderie of the staffroom in those few moments when they are not in the classroom or filling in forms. It is high time that we broke the individualistic mould in which we train our clergy and expect them to work, and replaced it with a more collegiate and communal environment. There is something deeply unchristian about the possessive individualism which characterises so many clergy and leads them to talk about 'my church', 'my congregation' and 'my kirk session/parochial church council'.

What is needed to turn a deanery synod, presbytery, ministers' fraternal or local council of churches into a *monasterium*? First and foremost a resolve to develop collaborative patterns of ministry, to acknowledge and give rein to different gifts and talents, to come together for regular worship and to witness together to Christ through commitment to a shared set of disciplines and mutual accountability. In this respect, modern management techniques of quality control, accountability, peer assessment and setting benchmarks and standards are marching in step with some of the key principles of Celtic monasticism. As someone who has not been generally very enthusiastic about the importation of management techniques into the workings of the Church, I have come to see that they may, in fact, when sensitively and imaginatively applied, help to promote the kind of shared ethos and discipline that was found in the monasteries of early medieval Britain and Ireland. They might also help to tackle some of the sense of isolation and failure felt by so many ministers today.

If we are to develop new 'colonies of heaven' on the model of the Celtic and Anglo-Saxon monastic communities, we also need to identify and promote places which can become the bases of the new-style *monasteria*. At the very least, these need to have facilities for members of the dispersed monastic/ministerial community to meet and pray together. Ideally, they should be places which can also offer hospitality in some form, be developed as educational and resource centres and provide sacred space and sanctuary and the regular rhythm of prayer and worship. Already several of these functions are being provided by individual church buildings. If anything, the problem is that we have too many church buildings, even active ones, often duplicating what others are doing. The business of closing churches is very painful, but in not taking this option huge strains are put on the finances, energies and time of many congregations. Most of our existing church buildings are not, like those of our Celtic

Christian ancestors, provisional and temporary. We are saddled, for better or worse (and in many ways it is for better), with the legacy of the Normans and their successors, who believed in building magnificent stone temples to God designed to last for hundreds of years. There are many fine churches which would make ideal bases for the new *monasteria*, particularly as places of regular prayer and worship. There are others for which it would be better to find alternative uses.

It is unrealistic in our culture of choice and diversity to imagine that we may get back to the notion of one church serving the whole community, but that does not mean that we should shrink from the painful task of cutting waste and duplication and concentrating resources on developing the modern equivalents of minsters and mother kirks. We need to be prepared to let churches die. Too many are at present kept going with the equivalent of artificial life-support systems that should now be switched off. Churches which can serve as the hubs of modern monastic families should be built up and supported. Radiating out from them, like the spokes of a wheel, would be cells, house churches and other groups probably operating out of more provisional and temporary premises. Not the least attractive feature of the *monasterium* model is that it allows the new predominantly evangelical and charismatic independent fellowships and churches to be integrated and linked to older established and more traditional denominations. As the former grow and the latter decline, there is indeed a strong case for redistributing buildings from the old to the new. As with closing churches, this will be a painful exercise, although it is surely better to hand over a much-loved place of worship to another more vibrant Christian group than to see it turned into a second-hand furniture depot or themed nightclub. The death and resurrection motif which stands at the heart of Christianity is as relevant to buildings and structures as to other aspects of the faith.

Developing modern *monasteria* with clusters of cells and satellite groups based around central or minster churches could promote an integrative and unifying ecclesiology at a time when so many current pressures tend towards splitting and fragmentation. A *monasterium* model would allow different styles of worship and churchmanship to flourish and be affirmed in the context of an extended family bound together by an overriding collegiality and common commitment. While the hub churches might maintain liturgical tradition, others in the monastic family could be involved in alternative worship. New churches and old, charismatic and traditional, liberal and conservative, would be held together by the provision of a broad-based ministry team reflecting different theological and liturgical styles, working from a central resource base and sharing a communal perspective while operating in a variety of different styles and locations.

At its best, the traditional parish church, perhaps even more than the monastery, provided a universal ministry of presence by being the one place of worship in the community. Except in a few largely rural areas, this situation no longer pertains, not just because of the existence of competing denominations but thanks to much greater mobility and the development of the consumer mentality among worshippers. It is quite common now for that diminishing segment of the population which does still go to church on Sunday to bypass, almost literally, their local parish church and drive several miles to a church which suits their own particular tastes and preferences in terms of churchmanship, style of worship, time of service or whatever. This is, as it were, the demand side, which is contributing to the demise of the parish system perhaps even more rapidly and effectively than the supply side of declining finances and clergy numbers. Social mobility, the breakdown of a sense of geographical community and the primacy of individual choice and consumer preference in our culture have combined to make most churches essentially gathered congregations.

There is another aspect of the contemporary culture of consumer choice which may actually help to promote the rediscovery of the monastery model from the demand side. We may balk at the ecclesiastical equivalent of the out-of-town hypermarket where everything is bigger and better than the corner shop but this is what churchgoers are increasingly demanding. Worshippers accustomed to the carefully rehearsed and professionally produced hymn-singing on *Songs of Praise* and the meticulously crafted cadences of broadcast sermons are often understandably disappointed by both the singing and the preaching in their local churches. The Celtic and Anglo-Saxon monasteries were centres of liturgical, artistic, pastoral and scholarly excellence. There is every reason to develop similar centres of excellence now which will serve both as places of creative and high-quality worship and pastoral care to which people will come for inspiration, refreshment and healing and also as bases from which ministerial teams can be equipped and resourced for worship, mission, teaching and pastoral care in other places. This process is already happening in the Church of England in several rural areas where, following the path of retail and service organisations in centralising operations in larger settlements and market towns, the 'minster model' of pastoral reorganisation is being adopted with ministry teams supporting smaller parishes.

In a way, of course, this is the role that cathedrals have traditionally exercised. As successors to the minsters, they have especially provided liturgical excellence, but have also offered other resources to daughter churches throughout their dioceses. Their constitutions have emphasised the communal dimension of cathedral life with their administration being in the hands of a dean and chapter of canons or *canonici*, a word which may well derive from the Greek word *koinonikoi* with its connotations of community and the common life. Sadly, recent episodes in the life of several English cathedrals have hardly suggested they are the most collegiate and communal of institutions, but there is some imaginative new thinking going on which, coupled with reforms being made in their form of government, suggests that they may be open and ready to take on something at least of the mantle of the Celtic monastery in the twenty-first century.

A recent collection of essays edited by Stephen Platten, Dean of Norwich, and Christopher Lewis, Dean of St Albans, under the title *Flagships of the Spirit*, while not specifically taking up the Celtic *monasterium* model, both acknowledges and seeks to recapture the monastic vision at the root of England's cathedrals. Christopher Rowland, Professor of the Exegesis of Holy Scripture at Oxford University, suggests that at its heart was 'a way of life in which worship and welfare were, in theory, closely interwined, warts and all', and notes that 'the remnants of those old monastic communities, which form the closes of many of our cathedrals, testify to that monastic ideal of divine service in the worship of lips and lives, devoted in practical service, the latter being in no way inferior to the former'.[14] Nicolas Alldrit, rector of a group of parishes in the Lincoln diocese, takes the monastic

model further in terms of the cathedral's relations
with those around it:

> The monastic tradition in its various forms is a
> quarry in which may be discovered appropri-
> ate models of community for today. Those
> who live in the vicinity of cathedrals should
> consider adopting some form of 'rule', which
> would include common worship and prayer,
> meeting together to discuss matters of com-
> mon concern, and mutual pastoral care . . .
> Then the life of a cathedral community will
> extend to care for others who are not of that
> immediate circle — as monastic life did in the
> past and does in the present . . . It is a model
> of the church that looks outwards, rather than
> inwards into a self-contained community
> bound by the needs of the cathedral itself.[15]

In their conclusion the two editors suggest an
essentially counter-cultural role for cathedrals, based
on a distinguishing hallmark that they share with the
Celtic and Anglo-Saxon monasteries, as places of
much coming and going:

> A cathedral is not only a place to which people
> come. It is also a place through which they go,
> and from which they emerge renewed. It is a
> place of interaction, between people and with
> God: not in order to escape from the world
> around, but rather to renew commitment to it.[16]

[31]

The Church of England has been at the forefront of thinking about these kinds of roles for cathedrals, but it is important that they are not just confined to Anglican institutions. There are Roman Catholic and Church of Scotland cathedrals, several of the latter in particular built on the sites of Celtic monasteries, which could act as mother kirks and be developed on the *monasterium* model. There are also plenty of parish churches and other church buildings, old and new, which could become bases for various kinds of modern *monasterium* – indeed, in some circumstances it may be most appropriate for a number of churches collectively to fulfil this role. Local circumstances will throw up very different kinds of building to function as the equivalents of the monastic *hospitium, scriptorium* and focal place of prayer.

Already around the country institutions of various kinds are being developed to fulfil functions very similar to some of those performed by the Celtic monasteries and specifically to cater for the burgeoning interest in spirituality and retreats. The Sarum Institute, set up in the magnificent house in Salisbury Cathedral close formerly occupied by a theological college, is a good example. It is the base for institutes of spirituality, liturgy and contemporary values and for the Southern Ordination Training Scheme as well as housing a well-used theological library and resource centre for church music. Its staff, who include ordained and lay Roman Catholics, Anglicans, Methodists and members of the United

Reformed Church, meet together regularly for meals and worship. The Institute also provides overnight accommodation for up to fifty guests and hosts a wide variety of courses, seminars and quiet days. The Mirfield Centre in West Yorkshire, which is closely linked to both the theological college and the Community of the Resurrection and provides a base for the interdenominational Northern Ordination Scheme, is taking on a similar role.

We need more places like these where people can explore spirituality, liturgy, missiology, pastoral care and other issues of contemporary Christian concern in an atmosphere of prayer and devotion rather than just of academic study. There are huge numbers of diploma and degree courses on these subjects offered and validated by all manner of academic institutions. Yet not everyone is afflicted with the modern disease of degree-itis and qualification-bagging – many simply want to explore and deepen their faith in a prayerful atmosphere. Ray Simpson tells of a seeker who came to Lindisfarne after visiting a Buddhist monastery. There, he said, he had been given a path to follow, taught how to meditate, learned how to be gentle towards the earth and offered a whole way of life. In Christian churches, by contrast, all he had found was a lot of ritual and a lot of words. I suppose he was lucky that he had not wandered into one of the many institutions now providing MA courses in spirituality – there he would have found more words and an emphasis on gaining credits and acquiring qualifications. We need more places where people can go, as they went to the Celtic monasteries, simply to sit at the feet of wise guides and to engage in study and meditation for its own sake. Such seeker-friendly establishments do exist, like the drop-in theological resource centre established by Elizabeth Templeton in Edinburgh, but they are few and far between. Perhaps this is something that could be taken on by retired people. A recovery of the role of elders as repositories of spiritual wisdom and discernment would be profoundly counter-cultural in our increasingly youth-oriented society but well worth exploring and supporting.

More important than buildings, of course, are the people brought together as a community of common intent and shared witness. Here again, flexibility and variety should be the keynote just as they were in the Celtic monasteries. The modern *monasterium* might consist of an ecumenical team ministry operating out of a town centre church (or churches), or it might be made up of a parochial church council, kirk session, deacon's court or similar body within an individual congregation (or group of congregations). The *monasterium* model could be applied across churches and denominations or within particular congregations. In the latter case, it might be expressed by the creation of a group whose members undertook to follow a certain lifestyle, subject themselves to certain rules and maintain a regular discipline of prayer and worship which would act as a central core and focus for the Christian life of the congregation as whole. Such a body could easily be grafted on to existing structures — those denominations which have elders, already recognised as being ordained and set apart for certain kinds of ministry and service, for example, should have no great difficulty in developing the *monasterium* model. There might well be different levels of commitment and varying rules, just as there were in Celtic monasteries. What there should definitely be, as in the Celtic and Anglo-Saxon *monasterium*, is the acknowledgement and affirmation of a wide variety of gifts and types of ministry.

In his interesting book *Celtic Gifts* Robert van de Weyer advocates the creation of different orders of ministry — the Order of St Aidan for bishops and archdeacons, the Order of St Cuthbert for pastors, the Order of St Patrick for preachers, the Order of St Brigid for healers, the Order of St Columba for artists and the Order of Iltut for administrators.[17] In his imaginary scenario, these orders begin life in a single Church of England diocese and are later taken up by other denominations and become fully ecumenical. In many ways it is an attractive vision although it may be too compartmentalised. Development of team ministries on the *monasterium* model would undoubtedly encourage the emergence of more specialist ministers concentrating on a particular area like liturgy, pastoral care or teaching. It would be sad, however, if this led to narrowly focused clergy who lacked the breadth of the 'jacks of all trades' produced in the parish-based system. Narrow specialism is certainly not the Celtic model of ministry. Monks moved from the *scriptorium* to the kitchens, mixing manual, intellectual and spiritual labour and always maintaining the balance between engagement in the world and withdrawal from it.

There is one key area of ministry where contemporary social trends create a need and Celtic monasticism provides a model for a more specialised and less generalised approach. Increasing mobility, fragmentation and consumer consciousness in society mean that people see themselves less and less as belonging to particular places and geographical communities and define their identity rather in terms of their work, their leisure interests and their age group. Nowadays the people in my community may not live anywhere near me. My community may span a sprawling metropolis, an entire country or may even, thanks to telephone, e-mail and the internet, have a global dimension. Increasingly people are united not by geographical proximity but by shared interests, reading the same magazines, watching the same TV shows, hitting the same sites on the web or going to the same club or bar. We live in an increasingly tribal and segmented world of niche marketing, theming and targeting where old bonds created by geographical proximity are fast breaking down.

As we have seen, Celtic monasteries, unlike parish churches, did not serve geographically defined areas but rather communities linked by ties of kinship and clan. The modern equivalent of this 'tribal' church is surely what is sometimes called sector ministry and more widely known as chaplaincy. This type of ministry, specifically targeted to reach and serve distinct communities, has spread in new and exciting ways over recent decades beyond its traditional loci in hospitals, armed forces, prisons and educational establishments. There are now chaplains to airports, shopping centres and leisure complexes as well as to specific occupational groups like farmers, those working in the offshore oil industry and police and ambulance personnel. More radically, churches seeking to reach out to teenagers and those in their twenties and early thirties are developing highly specialist ministries targeted at particular age and interest groups. St Cuthbert's Church in Edinburgh has recently taken on three full-time youth workers specifically to get alongside those involved in the city's clubbing culture. The inspiration for this particular initiative has come in part from Celtic monasticism and the model that it offers for those seeking to minister to the increasingly tribalised youth cultures of today.

Underlying these new initiatives in the field of sector ministry and chaplaincy is something of that notion of the ministry of presence that I have identified as being central to the role of the Celtic monastery. For most of the second millennium that ministry has been exercised primarily through the presence of parish churches and clergy across the country. As we move away from this model, we need

to be sure that we do not lose a sense of the importance of maintaining a ministry of presence, albeit in
very different (and perhaps more effective) ways than
in the past. In my book on Columba, I suggested that
the dominant ethos of the Columban church was one
of witness rather than mission. I also suggested that
the understanding of the Church as a presence within the community which went along with this provides a helpful ecclesiological model today when we
have perhaps become over-obsessed in churches as in
secular organisations with mission.

Extending generous hospitality to visitors, penitents
and local people was, as we have seen, one
of the most tangible ways in which the Celtic
monasteries expressed their ministry of presence. This
is a form of ministry which is being rediscovered by
many churches in different ways. Some have opened
up naves to provide an area in which meals can be
served and where playgroups can meet. Others use
their premises to provide day centres for the elderly.
The United Reformed Church in Bromley-by-Bow
houses a health centre. Increasingly church buildings
are being used not just for worship once or twice on a
Sunday but throughout the week for a whole range of
social and community activities. A neighbourhood
centre built around Orbiston Parish Church in
Lanarkshire as a result of the initiative of a small 'urban
theology group' in the congregation now employs
seventeen staff and thirty volunteers, opens from eight
in the morning until late every evening and provides

day-care facilities, mother and toddler groups, out-of-school care, arts and crafts workshops, exercise classes, counselling, a credit union, a food co-operative and an all-day café for over a thousand people a week in an area of high unemployment and poverty. In Ilford a number of churches have got together and open their premises on a rota basis as night shelters for the homeless. In other areas churches have become emergency drop-in centres and places of safety for victims of domestic violence and abuse. Offering this kind of hospitality to the vulnerable and damaged is immensely draining and demanding. Perhaps the biggest challenge that we now face in this area is in ministering to the mentally ill, now mostly without the support of psychiatric hospitals and left to the inadequacies of community care. It is clear that Celtic monasteries provided short-term and possibly also long-term sanctuary and asylum to those whom we would now diagnose as suffering from depression, schizophrenia and other mental illnesses. Providing this level of care today is perhaps only possible for dedicated therapeutic communities, but ordinary churches are already providing a ministry of hospitality for these people in a more basic way. A recent survey revealed that the mentally ill see the Church as the most supportive group in the community after their friends. A third of those questioned were in weekly contact with a church and their comments included 'I like their singing', 'They help me when I'm unwell' and 'They are very friendly people'.[18]

At an even simpler level, perhaps the most important ministry of hospitality that churches can provide is, like the Celtic monasteries, to be always open for people to drop in for a few quiet moments of prayer, contemplation and refreshment. Sadly the rising tide of vandalism and theft has meant that increasingly rural as well as urban churches are being locked up through the week. We desperately need to be able to open up all our churches so that they are available for those seeking a time of quiet reflection and sanctuary. Sterling work is being done by organisations like Scotland's Churches Scheme and Lord Lloyd Webber's Open Churches Scheme. The churches should not be shy of seeking financial support for this or other purposes from wealthy patrons. This is, after all, exactly what happened in the golden age of Celtic Christianity when monasteries were endowed and kept going entirely through the financial support of kings and rich nobles. Churches have perhaps become over-coy about having a relationship with the rich and powerful as well as with the poor and marginalised. We need to recover the strong links that Celtic monasteries had with rulers and wealth creators. The journalist Simon Jenkins has argued for new forms of both public and private ownership of church buildings if churches are to become arts and community centres as well as places of worship.

The ability of the Church to mobilise that degree of local patronage has gone. People now regard the church as the house of a sect, not the centre of their community. Many churches are now in very prosperous areas, whatever anybody says. There has to be a way of mobilising these people to support their churches and carry them forward, in my terms, as centres of community and centres of art.[19]

In our enthusiasm for creating multi-purpose churches, we should not forget that the central function of the Celtic monastery was as a house of prayer. So it should be for those buildings which become the bases for the new-style *monasteria* today. The recovery of the daily office has been a significant feature of the liturgical life of several denominations in the last decade or so and in several towns there is now at least one church where worship takes place every weekday. In keeping with its role as a modern *monasterium*, the neighbourhood centre attached to Orbiston Parish Church has a short act of worship each day at 1.30 p.m. Several of the churches in the City of London provide lunchtime weekday services for office workers and the City Churches Development Group has set aside one church for a monastic community who, it hopes, will follow the monastic hours of prayer, offer counselling and 'provide a still centre of quietness in the City'.[20]

Is 'monastery' the right term to use for these exciting new ways of being church that are already appearing at the dawning of the third millennium? I am all too aware that it still raises all sorts of Protestant hackles and conjures up images of monks shut off from society and sunk in unhealthy introspection. This negative view is nowhere better expressed than in Victor Hugo's epic novel *Les Misérables*:

> In the light of history, reason and truth,
> monastic life stands condemned . . .
> Monasteries, when they are numerous in a
> country, are knots in the circulation; encum-
> brances, centres of indolence, where there
> should be centres of industry. Monastic com-
> munities are to the great social community
> what the ivy is to the oak, what the wart is to
> the human body. Their prosperity and fatness
> are the impoverishment of the country.[21]

Hugo is of course thinking primarily of the monastic culture of medieval and post-medieval Continental Catholicism, characterised by 'the cloister filled with the black effulgence of death . . . mouths closed, brains walled-up, so many hapless intellects incarcerated in the dungeons of eternal vows'.[22] This is not the impression given in the surviving accounts that we have of Celtic monasticism. There is no doubt that there was a life-denying aspect to the life of the Irish monks. They were austere and ascetic to a degree that seems almost masochistic by our easygoing standards and, indeed, that disturbed the twentieth-century American Roman Catholic monk, Thomas Merton. In other respects an enthusiast for Celtic Christianity, he felt that while Celtic monasticism had a strange beauty, it was 'not always the beauty of the Gospel', being based on essentially Old rather than New Testament values and too full of 'legalist and ascetic rigorism'.[23] Yet it is hard to believe that the atmosphere in communities which produced the Book of Kells and the hermit poems was one of narrow legalism and morbid introspection.

The lengthy meditation on monasticism in *Les Misérables* comes at the point in the story where Jean Valjean and Cosette find sanctuary in the Convent of the Petit Picpus Sainte Antoine after jumping down from a tree into its garden in their efforts to escape from Inspector Javert. For all his rationalism and anti-clericalism, even Hugo is forced to concede that the chanting of the nuns which the two fugitives hear as they 'fall from heaven' sounds like the singing of angels and to acknowledge the mysterious power and efficacy of the continual prayer offered up in the convent. Indeed, he has a vivid appreciation of the monastery's role as a colony of heaven, describing it as

> that singular place, from which, as from the
> summit of a lofty mountain, we perceive, on
> one side, the abyss in which we are, and, on
> the other, the abyss wherein we are to be: it is

a narrow and misty boundary that separates
two worlds, where the unfeebled ray of life
commingles with the uncertain ray of death.[24]

For Hugo, the sense of standing between this world
and the next is the defining characteristic of those
called to the monastic life,

> those humble yet august souls, who dare to
> live upon the very confines of the great mys-
> tery, waiting between the world closed to them
> and heaven not yet opened; turned towards the
> daylight not yet seen, with only the happiness
> of thinking that they know where it is, their
> aspirations directed towards the abyss and the
> unknown, their gaze fixed on the motionless
> gloom, kneeling, stupefied, shuddering, and
> half borne away at certain times by the deep
> pulsations of Eternity.[25]

How do we begin to keep in time with the deep
pulsations of Eternity and establish colonies of
heaven in a society that is profoundly earthbound,
materialistic and secular? One way is by establishing
communities which embrace many of the disciplines
of monasticism and have a resident group at their
core, but which also attract substantial numbers of
adherents who do not practise communal living. The
development of such communities, and their
growing appeal, has been one of the most striking
and heartening features of Christian renewal in the

British Isles and elsewhere in recent times. The word 'community' has none of the negative overtones of 'monastery'. I suspect that it is rather overused but there is no doubt that it resonates with many people and their unease with a society that has become altogether too atomised, individualistic and self-centred.

Two communities first established more than sixty years ago on a consciously monastic model continue to exert a considerable impact today. The Taizé community set up in 1940 by Brother Roger now has over a hundred monks committed to vows of celibacy, obedience and community of material and spiritual goods, and offers hospitality to thousands of predominantly young people each year. It is centred around daily worship and has had a significant influence on both Protestant and Catholic liturgy, notably in the widespread adoption of its chants. The Iona Community, founded in 1938 by George MacLeod, is more consciously based on the model of Celtic monasticism and maintains a resident community engaged in daily worship, hospitality, education and service on the site of Columba's foundation on Iona. Unlike Taizé, however, it is essentially a dispersed community with its headquarters in Glasgow and its members scattered throughout the British Isles but bound together by their commitment to a common lifestyle and liturgy.

It is very tempting to see George MacLeod as a latter-day reincarnation of Columba. The two men had much in common: aristocratic antecedents, com-

manding and charismatic characters which made
them natural if somewhat autocratic leaders, a profound mystical streak and personalities which combined stubborn pride with deep humility and an
almost childlike simplicity and enthusiasm. Life on
Iona in the early days of the community was much as
it must have been for Columba's monks, all-male,
highly disciplined and strongly inclined towards
muscular Christianity with dips in the cold sea before
breakfast. These aspects have disappeared, but
MacLeod's burning commitment to social justice and
peace and his interest in liturgical renewal have continued to inform the life of the Iona Community. Its
current activities are well described in a recently
published book by Norman Shanks, the present
leader, Iona — God's Energy: The Spirituality and Vision of the
Iona Community. The Iona Community currently has
211 members, over 1,500 associate members,
around 1,700 friends and three main bases. On Iona
a resident group and shorter-term volunteers based
in the restored Abbey buildings and adjoining
MacLeod Centre provide innovative morning and
evening worship, host residential weeks on aspects of
theology, spirituality and political and social issues,
and also provide hospitality for numerous day visitors and pilgrims. The remote Camas centre on Mull
caters especially for groups with special needs and
from disadvantaged situations. Offices in Glasgow
house the leader and administrative staff and members of the Wild Goose Resource group, much

involved in song writing and promoting liturgical renewal in both the United Kingdom and abroad.

The Iona Community reverses the usual pattern of monastic life in that those working in its (literally) cloistered heart do not necessarily share the commitment to its monastic principles of those who are physically far away from it. The full-time staff, of whom there are over fifty running the day-to-day life of its centres, are not necessarily members of the community. Most of the community's members work and live far away from Iona or Glasgow. They are not monks in the sense of living together and sharing in the work of the *monasterium* but they do take vows and agree to follow a demanding fivefold rule. To become a member takes two years and involves following a programme which is deliberately designed to resemble a religious order's novitiate in terms of testing commitment and exploring the compatibility of the hopes of the individual and the concerns of the community. Once enrolled, members undertake to read the Bible regularly and frequently and to pray for each other, for their shared concerns and for the wider work of the Church on a daily basis, using a lectionary produced by the Community under the title *Miles Christi*. They also agree to share and account for the use of money and to give away 10 per cent of their disposable income. The third element in the fivefold rule involves sharing and accounting for the use of time and picks up the central Celtic monastic themes of balance and rhythm by requiring members to plan their time in such a way that proper weighting is given to work, leisure, time with family, developing skills and acquiring new ones, worship and devotion, voluntary work and rest and sleep. The fourth rule commits members to involving themselves in action for justice and peace, and they are also required to meet regularly with each other in local family groups and plenary sessions. All such meetings begin with the recitation of the Community's office.

Over the years the Iona Community has explored several ways of being the church in modern society. One of the most interesting in terms of the *monasterium* model has been the planting of Columban houses in deprived and inner-city areas. Originally set up in the mid-1980s on an experimental basis, several of these houses are still in existence, offering a model of communal living and Christian witness in which a group of usually young people live together in a tenement flat or council house, exercising what is often a very demanding ministry of presence in areas where there is often little in the way of church life or activity. The Columban houses are indeed 'colonies of heaven' in a very real sense.

The Community of Aidan and Hilda is a much more recent and as yet much smaller operation. Launched in 1994 at an Anglican Renewal Conference in Swanwick by a group of charismatic Anglicans led by Ray Simpson and Michael Mitten, it currently has 23 members and 96 explorers spread across the United Kingdom with a few more overseas. Its main base on Lindisfarne is a recently acquired community and retreat house, the Open Gate, with a resident husband-and-wife team as wardens assisted by short-term volunteers. The Community's guardian, Ray Simpson, also runs a smaller retreat centre in his cottage in the main square. The Open Gate provides a rhythm of morning and night prayer, simple accommodation for guests and a ministry of welcome to enquirers. It is hoped that eventually it will form the base of a larger community run along the lines of a Celtic hermitage in which members will be self-supporting and have their own dwelling and work but come together for daily prayer, weekly meals and meetings.

More self-consciously Celtic in its inspiration and structures than the Iona Community, the Community of Aidan and Hilda proclaims its purpose as 'the cradling of a Christian spirituality for today inspired by the Celtic saints'. Its three main aims are to restore the memory and experience of the Church in the period of the first Celtic mission in ways that relate to God's purposes today and bring healing to the land; to research the history, spirituality and relationship to cultural patterns of the Celtic mission and how these apply to the renewal of today's church and society; and to resource, through the provision of materials for prayer, worship and study, personal and group retreats, workshops and networking with link churches and centres. Like the Iona Community, it is essentially a dispersed community with most members living a good distance away from its Lindisfarne base. This feature is seen as being in accordance with the Celtic monastic tradition:

> In the early Celtic church there were those who lived within the monastic boundary as part of the physical community but there were also ascetics and missionaries who lived outside the Community but who were still regarded as part of it. Our modern situation is similar but in reverse. Only a few of us are able to live in physical community on Lindisfarne. The rest of us live as pilgrims, pastors or missionaries in the places to which God has called us but we still belong together because we are rooted in the Community and share the Way of Life.[26]

As with the Iona Community, there are three different levels of adherence to the Community of Aidan and Hilda, representing varying degrees of commitment. Those simply wishing to support the community become friends. Those interested in rather greater involvement and commitment are enrolled as explorers and are given the assistance of a soul friend as they seek over a period of a year to test their vocation and draft a personal rule of life. If they feel called to become full members they take vows committing themselves to following the community's way of life for a year, a step which is known as taking the first voyage of the coracle. Those ready to make a lifetime commitment subsequently take the long voyage of the coracle.

The community's way of life is based on the monastic principles of poverty, chastity and obedience. It has ten aspects — study and application of the Celtic Christian way which involves daily Bible reading and study of the history of the Celtic Church; spiritual journey, involving meeting with a soul friend at least twice a year, going on regular retreats and making pilgrimages; a daily rhythm of prayer, work and rest; intercessory prayer, recognising the reality of the supernatural and spiritual warfare; simplicity of lifestyle; care for and affirmation of creation; wholeness rather than fragmentation, involving the encouragement of the ministry of Christian healing; openness to the wind of the Spirit; unity and community; and mission.

In many ways these two dispersed communities complement each other, the former having a distinctly liberal theological hue and a strong interest in justice and peace issues, the latter being predominantly charismatic in outlook with a focus on spirituality and mission. Both are pioneering extremely interesting ways of applying the *monasterium* model today. While the Iona Community continues to fulfil its visionary founder's aim of 'finding new ways to touch the hearts of all', Ray Simpson has made the Community of Aidan and Hilda a focus for new thinking on how

characteristically Celtic themes like monastic discipline and soul friending can be applied to enrich the
life and mission of contemporary churches.

The last few decades have seen the founding of
many other Christian communities which, although
in most cases not directly inspired by the example of
Celtic monasticism, operate as modern-day *monasteria*
with resident groups of lay and ordained Christians
living together in community, celebrating daily worship and offering hospitality to visitors. The Pilsdon
Community in Dorset, founded in 1958, offers a
refuge to people in crisis and has opened its doors to
the homeless, alcoholics and drug addicts, asylum
seekers and those suffering from depression and
from physical disabilities. At its core is a small group
of Christians who have renounced a private home
and ordinary family life to create a household where
all are welcome. Central to its ethos, as to the life of
the Celtic monastery, is a balance of worship, held
daily in the small medieval church in the grounds,
and work, seen as a gift to the life of community, a
means of personal fulfilment and an offering to God.
Providing a similar combination of communal living
and sanctuary for the vulnerable and disadvantaged
are the Camphill villages, which follow the monastic
tradition of living close to the land by engaging in
organic agriculture, and the Emmaus communities,
originally started in France in 1949, and extended to
Britain in 1991. There are now seven Emmaus
communities in the British Isles, each providing both

a home and a workplace for twenty to thirty companions who are drawn from the ranks of the homeless. Other longer-standing small residential communities, such as those associated with St Deiniol's Library at Hawarden in north Wales, Rydal Hall, the Carlisle Diocesan Retreat Centre near Ambleside in the Lake District, Launde Abbey in Leicestershire, Lee Abbey in North Devon and Scargill House in North Yorkshire, provide a ministry of hospitality and a programme of retreats and courses on aspects of spirituality and faith grounded in a regular rhythm of prayer and devotion.

The growing number and increasing appeal of these and other similar communities, as places both to visit for a short time and to stay for longer periods, are in marked contrast to the decline in conventional church membership and attendance and in vocations to more closed monastic institutions. Could it be that this model of church as community is much more appropriate and appealing particularly to young people nowadays than the model of church as building and institution which has predominated through much of the second millennium? One of its key features is its flexibility. It does not need to have a resident core, although it almost certainly needs some base. The Quest Community, set up in Glastonbury in 1993, is a wholly dispersed community of Christians from a variety of different denominations who live in their own homes but meet together often for prayer, work and study and to share and offer hospitality and a listening ear. At the centre of its life are the daily prayers said at noon in the medieval chapel in Magdalene Street in the heart of a town which has become a mecca for New Age travellers and seekers of every kind.

Alongside and as part of this rediscovery of the value of community there is a growing interest among Christians in following a common rule of life. One of the most significant examples of this that I know of is the 'Living Way' practised by members of Christ Church, Epsom Common, in the midst of the Surrey commuter belt. It was developed in Lent 1992 by the then vicar, Mark Wilson, now Archdeacon of Dorking, responding to a general concern felt in the congregation 'to find some broad guidelines that offered a structure for mutual support as we worked out how to live as Christian disciples in today's individualistic culture'.[27] The Living Way covers four areas: relationship to God, personal lifestyle and responsibilities, relations with others and mission to the world. It involves a commitment to daily prayer and Bible reading, either by attending morning and evening prayer in the church or making time to read the set psalm and Scripture portion, responsible Christian stewardship of talents, possessions and finances, practising generosity and hospitality and sharing the gospel message and working for God's Kingdom. Around a hundred people, making up a third of the church's electoral roll, are currently following this rule of life and each one is supported by a soul companion.

Could it be that in the post-modern, pick-and-mix spiritual supermarket we now inhabit, people are actually craving commitment, discipline and obedience? What might seem at first sight to be one of the least appealing aspects of the *monasterium* model to modern Christians is perhaps an increasingly positive attraction. Norman Shanks notes in his new book that the demanding fivefold rule is one of the strongest 'selling points' of membership of the Iona Community, providing as it does 'the possibility of discipline within highly pressured lives'.[28] So great is now the demand for full membership that the Community has had to impose a ceiling of twenty-four new members a year. A high level of commitment is also, of course, one of the most striking characteristics of the membership of the growing house church and new church movement in Britain which, as we shall see in later chapters of this book, has other affinities with the practices and outlook of Celtic Christianity. Certainly in terms of both time and money, members of these new churches generally show a much higher level of commitment than those in the traditional declining churches. They often practise tithing, for example, giving 10 per cent of their income to the Church. The level of individual giving in the Church of England and Church of Scotland, by contrast, averages less than £2 a week.

Churches, like so many other institutions in our society, often have low expectations and make few demands of their members. Maybe in our dumbed down and easygoing culture Christians should be both proclaiming and living out the essentially counter-cultural message of commitment and discipline which is so clearly found in the Celtic and Anglo-Saxon *monasterium*. Ian Smith, a Baptist, has recently berated the Church of Scotland on this very point:

> When little is demanded from members, little is given. If commitment requires no more than occasional attendance at Communion, it is not surprising that the average level of participation among members is low. There are large numbers who belong and believe, but contribute very little. In order to grow – indeed, just to stand still – it is essential that the Church starts to tap and to mobilise these underutilised resources. The important thing is not only regular attendance at worship but involvement in church activities during the week. How can this level of commitment be achieved? The answer lies in inverting the first principle: when much is demanded from members, much is given.[29]

I hope it is not just my liberal established-church mentality that makes me want to sound a slight note of caution here. There is a danger of turning the

Church into a holy huddle and scaring away those who for whatever reason feel that they cannot make the commitment to join the inner sanctum. It may well be highly desirable for churches to build core groups of members who act as a kind of monasterium, perhaps sharing a common rule of life and disciplines of prayer. We should not forget, however, the variety of ministries found within the Celtic monastery which sprang from a recognition of different levels and expressions of commitment to Christ, as well as of different gifts and callings. The monasteria were essentially open communities, providing staging posts for seekers as well as homes to the committed. We should have this dual role and this sense of variety and balance in mind as we seek to plant our colonies of heaven today.

2

Blessing and Cursing

You cannot read far in the lives of the Celtic saints without being struck by how often they blessed people, places and even everyday objects. Columba, for example, is portrayed by his biographer Adamnan making the sign of the cross and invoking God's blessing on a fruit tree, a block of salt, a pail of milk and a small round stone from a river as well as on his monks and on the island of Iona and its inhabitants. Although many of these benedictions were associated with miraculous happenings and transformations, it is clear from what Adamnan writes that Columba also pronounced blessings on people and objects as a matter of routine and that many people made the long and potentially hazardous journey to Iona just to be blessed by the saint.

Blessings also seem to have had an important place in the worship of the early native Christian communities in the British Isles. The Antiphonary of Bangor, which may date back to the late seventh century and which is probably the earliest surviving collection of liturgical material from an Irish monastery, accords a prime place to the *Benedicite*, the canticle which calls on all the elements of God's creation to bless the Lord, from the stars of heaven, the showers and dew and the lightning and clouds to the whales, beasts, cattle and fowls of the air. According to some authorities, one of the distinctive features of the eucharistic liturgy celebrated in Ireland, and so by extension in Scotland, Wales and northern England, was the prominence and frequency of episcopal blessings during the course of the service.

This tradition of benediction is reflected in later Gaelic and Welsh sources and has, indeed, been one of the most marked characteristics of the continuing legacy of a distinctive Celtic Christianity in the religious life and literature of Ireland, Wales and the Scottish Highlands and islands over the last thirteen hundred years or so. It is perhaps most clearly discernible in the Welsh tradition of praise poems which has been lovingly celebrated and opened up for English readers in recent years by Donald Allchin, Oliver Davies, Fiona Bowie, Saunders and Cynthia Lewis and Brendan O'Malley. From the brief verse scribbled in the margin of a ninth-century Latin manuscript proclaiming that the world cannot express all God's glories, to Euros Bowen's 1984 poem 'Gloria' with its ringing affirmation that 'The whole world is full of God's glory' and that 'to curse life is to err', celebration of the goodness of God's creation has been a constant and dominant motif in Welsh language poetry.[1] Blessings figure prominently in the collections of Gaelic prayers and poems made in the late nineteenth century by Alexander Carmichael in the Hebrides and Douglas Hyde in Ireland. Carmichael's *Carmina Gadelica* in particular abounds with prayers invoking God's blessing on such routine daily tasks as lighting the fire, milking the cow and preparing for bed, reflecting a tradition which survived in the Western Isles until relatively recently. In rural Ireland, where people are still greeted with the phrase 'God be with you', the habit of pronouncing blessings has lingered to our own day.

The prominence of benediction in early British and Irish Christianity may have in part reflected an important aspect of pre-Christian Celtic culture. The Celts had a very strong sense of the almost physical power of the spoken word both to heal and to harm. The Irish *file* (poet) was thought to have two compartments in his tongue, one for honey and the other for poison. This was one of the main reasons why the Celts were so reluctant to write things down and maintained an almost exclusively oral tradition until Christian monks, imbued with the new religion of the book, began to commit to manuscript not just their own sacred Scriptures but the legends and lays of pre-Christian times. With the coming of Christianity, this belief in the force of the spoken word and its ability to work an almost tangible effect for good or ill was not extinguished but simply integrated into the new belief system. Its persistence among Christian hagiographers is well illustrated in the strange story recounted by Adamnan in which Columba causes a wild boar to collapse dead in front of him, killing it 'by the power of his terrible word'.[2]

With this understanding of the power of the spoken word, pronouncing a blessing or benediction was no mere pleasantry or routine greeting to pass the time of day. Nor did it simply involve, as its Latin root *benedicere* suggests, speaking well of someone or something. Rather it conveyed to the recipient in an almost physical sense a portion of God's goodness and grace. Blessings were carried out in the name of the Lord, generally included the recitation of some kind of trinitarian formula and often invoked the aid of Michael, the angels and archangels and specific saints. Although those delivered by saints and holy men were regarded as having a special force and efficacy, blessings were certainly not regarded as the exclusive province of priests and monks, and could come from the lips of any Christian. They were emphatically not confined to liturgical use but had a prominent place in the everyday lives and conversation of laity and clergy alike, both inside and beyond the monastic *vallum*.

Blessings were often directed at or invoked by

those who were in situations of danger, harm and suffering. In the Welsh language there is a distinctive genre of healing poems known as *cywydd* which illustrate very clearly the Celtic understanding of the therapeutic power of words. A good example is the poem composed in the fifteenth century by Gutor Glyn as, in Donald Allchin's words, 'a rather elaborate get well card' for Hywel of Moelyrch after the latter had injured his knee:

> The sound of the poetry of Taliesin
> Got his master out of prison.
> I have a mind, because of what I might
>   compose,
> To get the knee out of the prison of a wound.
> Many a person (you're golden-handed)
> Was healed with a *cywydd*.
> I swear by the fire, I too
> Will make an ointment of praise for you.
> And if the mouth (and what it made)
> Doesn't have the power of a medication,
> The host of heaven will make you merrily
>   well.[3]

This poem goes on to invoke over the wounded Hywel the blessings of Christ, Mary and the saints, specifically Silin, Oswald, Martin of Tours and Lednart, and ends with a promise that its author will sing no more 'bold praise poetry' until the patient walks again.

The Celtic saints used blessings of various kinds in the context of their own healing ministries. Adamnan records of Columba that 'many sick people put their trust in him and received full healing, some from his outstretched hand, some from being sprinkled with water he had blessed, others by the mere touching of the edge of his cloak, or from something such as salt or bread blessed by the saint and dipped in water'.[4] If this seems to smack of the world of the pagan medicine man and witch doctor, then it is also, of course, fully consistent with the Gospel stories of those who came to Jesus saying 'Speak the word only and thy servant shall be healed', and who found healing by touching his garment. Many of the blessings invoked by the Celtic saints are recorded in the context of the performance of a miracle. Pronouncing God's blessing and making the sign of the cross were often enough to turn something from evil to good and to frustrate or expel the devil. By these actions, according to Adamnan, Columba was able to turn the fruit of a tree from bitterness to sweetness, to cause water (for use in baptism) to flow from a barren rock face, to drive the devil out of a milk pail, and even to calm the fury of the Loch Ness monster. The miracles which accompanied or followed blessings by the saints often had a healing dimension. To take three further examples from Adamnan's life of Columba, a block of salt blessed by the saint for use in healing a man's eye was miraculously preserved when fire destroyed the house in which it was hanging, a man who had suffered a nosebleed for a month was cured when the saint blessed him while pinching his nostrils together, and the venom of snakes on Iona lost its poisonous effect on humans as a result of the saint's blessing.

This culture of blessing was part of a wider understanding of the spiritual warfare in which Christians were called to engage with the dark forces of sin and evil. In this battle, the invocation of God's power as well as of his love was vital if the forces of good were to prevail. This is why in the Irish tradition, particularly, so many prayers and poems of blessing speak of protecting and encircling. The best-known group of blessings which fall into this category are the so-called breastplate or *lorica* prayers which are, of course, strongly biblical in inspiration and borrow heavily from the passage in Ephesians 6:10–17 where Paul writes about putting on the whole armour of God. Another distinctive genre is the *caim* or encircling prayer, almost certainly deriving from a pre-Christian tradition of protective charms and incantations, which is recited as a protective circle is physically traced around one's person, family, home or community.

Many of these blessings invoking God's protection clearly belong to folk- rather than clerical tradition and were used by lay Christians in the course of their own daily encounters with difficulties and dangers rather than by priests in a liturgical context. As well as using striking military metaphors they are full of comfort and assurance. The words which crop up again and again are guarding, shielding, compassing and enfolding. The world that they portray, however, is anything but comfortable. It is full of dangers, dark corners and malevolent enemies. It is from these harmful influences that the *lorica* prayers call down God's protection. Nowhere are they spelt out in more detail than in the Irish prayer, which probably dates from the eighth or ninth century, known as St Patrick's Breastplate:

> from snares of the demons,
> from evil enticements,
> from failings of nature,
> from one man or many
> that seek to destroy me,
> anear or afar . . .
> from dark powers that assail me:
> against false prophesyings,
> against pagan devisings,
> against heretical lying
> and false gods all around me.
> Against spells cast by women,
> by blacksmiths, by Druids,
> against knowledge unlawful
> that injures the body,
> that injures the spirit.[5]

It is striking how many of the evils listed in this prayer involve the harm done by the spoken word, whether in the form of enticements, prophesyings, devisings, lying or spells.

A similar sense of the need for protection from the destructive power of words underlies several of the Gaelic poems collected and translated by Alexander Carmichael and published in the *Carmina Gadelica*, like this prayer recited by a crofter at Taynuilt near Oban:

> Thou Michael of militance,
> Thou Michael of wounding,
> Shield me from the grudge
> Of ill-wishers this night.
> Ill-wishers this night.
>
> Thou Christ of the tree
> Thou Christ of the cross,
> Snatch me from the snares
> Of the spiteful ones of evil,
> The spiteful ones of evil.[6]

We do not, in fact, need to look to pagan and pre-Christian influences when seeking the origins of this tradition of invoking God's protection and blessing in situations of potential harm and danger, and especially against the destructive power of words spoken in anger or malice. The Psalms are full of such prayers:

> Lead me and protect me, Lord,
> because I am beset by enemies;

give me a straight path to follow.
Nothing they say is true;
they are bent on complete destruction.
Their throats are gaping tombs;
smooth talk runs off their tongues.
God, bring ruin on them;
let their own devices be their downfall.

(Psalm 5: 8–10 REB)

While many of the Celtic blessings and encircling prayers clearly belong to a negative context of danger and suffering, it would be wrong to regard the wider tradition of benediction of which they were a part as being wholly rooted in a world-view which emphasised the theme of spiritual warfare between the forces of good and evil. Blessings were not simply applied as a kind of instant first aid to ward off adversaries and effect miracles which turned bad to good. They were also offered and sought in more positive situations in a way that was spontaeous and almost routine. Setting the scene for his bizarre story of the devil in the milk pail, Adamnan writes of a young man returning from milking his cows and stopping at Columba's hut to ask the saint to bless the pail 'according to his custom'.[7] Another of his stories indicates how common it was for things to be brought to Columba for blessing. So routine was it, in fact, that in this instance the saint did not bother to look up from the manuscript which he was copying and simply reached out his hand, still holding his pen, and made the sign of the cross over the object being presented to him. It was only later that he casually asked his servant what it was that he had blessed. On being told that it was a knife, Columba expressed his 'trust in my Lord that the implement I have blessed will not harm man or beast'.[8] This trust was, indeed, fulfilled as the knife proved unable to penetrate skin.

In so far as there was a Celtic theology of benediction underlying this almost matter-of- fact approach to blessing everything and everyone, it stemmed from an understanding of the redeemed nature of the world. Redemption is the key concept here. Matthew Fox, the contemporary Californian guru of creation spirituality, may be right to claim certain Celtic Christian figures like John Scotus Eriugena as early exponents of the notion of original blessing which he puts forward as a counter to the Augustinian obsession with original sin. I have myself suggested in The Celtic Way that there may have been a Pelagian strain in Celtic Christianity which took a more positive view of both human and physical nature than Augustine and his many followers in both the later Catholic and Reformed traditions. It is quite wrong, however, to identify Celtic Christianity with a world-view which is wholly benign and where there is no room for sin and evil. The many prayers for protection serve as a reminder that there was a very strong sense of the power of sin and of the almost tangible presence of dark and evil forces. Yet there was also a clear understanding that in coming in human form and setting his feet on the earth, Jesus Christ had redeemed the world and made it a changed place. Redemption was seen as an ongoing process rather than a completed and accomplished fact. Indeed, it required the active co-operation and work of Christians to fulfil and perfect it. The many stories attached to the lives of the Celtic saints which tell of them building monasteries on the sites of pagan shrines and temples, turning wells and springs dedicated to pagan deities into holy healing places, and outdoing the magic of druidic wizards with their own miracle working, point to the importance of this redemptive work in which, significantly, the action of pronouncing a blessing often played a vital role.

If the Celtic saints were concerned about redeeming people and places from their pagan past, then they were also very conscious that they lived in a world which had itself been redeemed by Christ from its slavery to sin and which was therefore in a very real sense a blessed place. This continuing dimension of the Celtic tradition of benediction was well identified by George Congreve, an Irish-born member of the Anglican monastic order, the Society of St John the Evangelist (better known as the Cowley Fathers), which occupied Bishop's House on Iona from 1897 to 1912:

I think you will find this characteristic still
surviving more markedly in Celtic Christianity
than in any other – this sense of living in a
world redeemed, in which the eternal Word,
taking a created nature, has become for every
creature a link with God. Every common thing
is regarded among the songs of St Patrick and
St Columba as in the blessing of God. Is it good
manners in Ireland among the peasants today
to name a friend without God bless him? If we
meet a man on the road and exchange a
friendly word about the weather, it must end
with Thank the Lord. The well is holy and the tree
that overshadows it; the field is blessed, and
the sea and the boat. Whoever forgot to make
the holy sign and to say grace before meat?
And is there not still somewhere at the lighting
of the evening rush-light in the cabin, the
grace for light?

And this sense of living in a redeemed
world, where every creature is his friend for
Christ's sake, sustains the Celt in joy which has
a real spiritual foundation, and that often
under circumstances which offer him little
material ground for hope. His religion gives
him a joyousness which belongs to his eternal
home, but which finds food for itself in everything here below, as he passes among his
creatures which share his high destiny, and
wish him Godspeed on the way.[9]

I want to go one step further than George Congreve did in that fascinating analysis, which was made in a speech on Iona in 1908, and suggest that the Celtic Christian tradition of benediction springs from a sense of living in a world which is not just redeemed but also sacramental in the sense that it is shot through with the glory of God, so that even the most mundane things are heavenly. A sacramental understanding of creation, which sees the world and all it contains as a great theophany or showing of God's glory, is not of course by any means confined to Celtic Christianity. It is to be found in Eastern Orthodoxy, in the writings of many mystics and perhaps most strikingly in the poems of the Jesuit Gerard Manley Hopkins. Yet it is a very distinctive strain in Celtic spirituality, so rightly characterised by John Macquarrie as having an intense sense of presence that is both 'God-intoxicated' and utterly down to earth.[10] We find it in the affirmation in the catechism attributed to Ninian that the fruit of all study is 'to perceive the eternal word of God reflected in every plant and insect, every bird and animal, and every man and woman', in the modern Irish poet Patrick Kavanagh's observation that 'among your earthiest words the angels stray' and in two of George MacLeod's favourite aphorisms, 'the glory in the grey' and 'turn but a stone and an angel moves'.[11] This sense of the sacramentality of creation pervades many of the verses in Carmichael's *Carmina Gadelica*:

There is no plant in the ground
But is full of His virtue,
There is no form in the strand
But is full of His blessing . . .

There is no life in the sea,
There is no creature in the river,
There is naught in the firmament,
But proclaims His goodness . . .

There is no bird on the wing,
There is no star in the sky,
There is nothing beneath the sun,
But proclaims His goodness . . . [12]

The goodness of God as proclaimed through his creation is a more marked theme in the Gaelic prayers of blessing collected by Carmichael in the nineteenth century than it is in the Irish prayers written a thousand or more years earlier. The later material, which reflects an altogether gentler and more benign world-view than that apparently held by Patrick, Columba and their immediate successors, displays a theology of prevenient grace, often using words like 'serenely' and 'generously' to describe the manner in which God's love is poured out over his creatures. In Welsh religious verse, as we have seen, celebration of the glory of God as demonstrated in the blessings of his creation has been a continuous theme from the early Christian centuries until the present day. Perhaps nowhere is it more beautifully expressed than in the thirteenth-century poem 'The Loves of Taliesin':

> The beauty of the virtue in doing penance for
>   excess,
> Beautiful too that God shall save me.
> The beauty of a companion who does not
>   deny me his company,
> Beautiful too the drinking horn's society.[13]

At one level, this poem operates like an extended set of Beatitudes, substituting 'beautiful' for 'blessed' and cataloguing the whole range of God's creation from 'the garden when the leeks grow well' to the pattern of the plaits on the neck of a thick-maned stallion. It also has a deeper message. As in the opening lines quoted above, so throughout the poem, worldly blessings like the drinking horn and the companionable friend are bracketed with spiritual blessings like the virtue of penance and the saving power of God. There is a great sense both of the interconnectedness of the sacred and secular and of their own intrinsic goodness. Oliver Davies, whose translations and commentaries have opened up the treasures of Welsh medieval religious poetry to English speaking readers, has written of how 'The Loves of Taliesin' draws together the so often separated realms of nature and grace:

It does so in a way that draws the glorious dimension out from what is merely beautiful. In other words, the juxtaposition of what is natural and divine, both encompassed by the words *atwyn* (literally 'a beautiful thing') and *arall atwyn* (lit. 'another beautiful thing') which alternately introduce every line of the poem, serves to suggest that the divine presence is everywhere, at all levels of human experience and life, just as it is present also in the natural world. The 'Loves of Taliesin' then represents a truly cosmic vision of God's glory, which knows no boundaries.[14]

Donald Allchin, another modern commentator who has been struck by the theme of blessing in the Welsh praise poems, feels that in this tradition there is a great affinity between the roles of poet and priest:

> Both are called, in different ways, to bless; and to bless (*benedicere*) in its original meaning is to speak good things, to declare the goodness which is latent in the world around us, when that world is seen and known as the world of God . . . As poets, all human beings are called to be co-workers with God, co-creators. We are called to discern and proclaim the latent goodness of the creation around us and within us. As priests we are called to offer that goodness back to God in a movement

of praise and thanksgiving which is at the same time a movement of intercession and concern.[15]

It is misleading to think of Celtic Christians as 'beautiful people' always full of sweetness and light who went round saying nice things about each other. The Celtic tradition of benediction had its obverse side in a tradition of malediction. Celtic saints were renowned for their propensity to curse as well as to bless. Giraldus Cambrensis, the late-twelfth-century chronicler, famously observed that Irish and Welsh saints seemed to be possessed of a particular vindictive nature in their talent for cursing. Whilst this activity was certainly not confined to Celtic Christians – a recently published monograph is entitled *Benedictine Maledictions – Liturgical Cursing in Romanesque France* – scholars are agreed that references to cursing are far more frequent in the lives of Irish and Welsh saints than in other medieval hagiography. Cursing Welsh saints included David, who banished bees from the settlement of one of his followers and withered the hand of a man who was about to strike him, Cadog, who caused a servant guilty of insubordination to be burned to death in a barn and occasioned the death of two disciples when they carelessly left his book behind on Flatholm, and Germanus, who dispatched several enemies to die through fire. The cursing power of the Welsh saints remained strong even after death: a ruler who refused to believe in

Illtud's body and altar lost his life. Several stories in Adamnan's life of Columba describe the saint's prayers leading to the death of evildoers. In one, he tells a man who has just killed a girl that in the same hour that her soul ascends to heaven, his shall descend to hell. 'He had no sooner spoken', records Adamnan, 'than that slaughterer of innocents fell dead on the spot.'[16]

In several cases the 'curses' uttered by Celtic saints can be seen as prophetic rebukes to those who have abused their power and wealth. Bede notes of Aidan, for example, that 'if wealthy people did wrong, he never kept silent out of respect or fear, but corrected them outspokenly'.[17] In other instances, however, the saints' propensity to strike dead those who have annoyed them seems rather vindictive and cruel. Yet once again it has good biblical precedent. The Book of Psalms, so central to both public and private devotion in the monasteries of Ireland, Scotland, Wales and northern England, is full of curses:

> He loved to curse:
> may the curse recoil on him!
> He took no pleasure in blessing:
> may no blessing be his!
>
> Happy is he who repays you
> for what you did to us!
> Happy is he who seizes your babes
> and dashes them against a rock.[18]

Cursing saints are one aspect of Celtic Christianity that we surely do not want to revive today. Or may they, in fact, have something to say to us in our mealy-mouthed and platitudinous culture? For a church that believes in the primacy of the Word, and the Word made flesh, we are pretty unimaginative in our use and choice of words. We certainly use them in plenty – too many in most of our services – but they lack the power of the blessings and cursings of the Celtic saints. So often we strive not to give offence and not to say what we really mean, hiding our true feelings beneath a polite, smooth, non-committal banter.

There is already a move afoot to change this and to liberate Christians to be more honest and direct in their vocabulary, even if this means being angry as well as meek and mild. John Bell, leader of the Iona Community's Wild Goose Worship Group, is particularly keen that we should rehabilitate those sections of the Psalms that have been excised from modern use because we find them too strong and they jar with our desire not to offend. He points out that many people find themselves in the position of the author of Psalm 5 (quoted on pp.66–7), the victims of slander and gossip. It is quite appropriate, he thinks, for such people to utter curses and put the matter into God's hands. 'God wants us to be honest, not to be nice' he says. On the whole, the Church does not allow people to vent their anger. Yet expressing anger can be very important for someone's healing and wholeness. There are many people in our society who feel that they have had a curse put upon them – by abuse in childhood or later, violence from a partner or a wounding remark made that they have never forgotten. It is important that, like the authors of the Psalms, they can articulate their anger against those who have made their lives a misery and not simply allow it to fester.[19]

Cursing may also be an appropriate response when we are confronted with manifest evil at an institutional or social level. Racism is a clear case in point where Christians have denounced attitudes and practices in a manner that is not very different from Aidan's rebukes to the oppressive rulers of his day. Pastoral rebuke is perhaps a better term for this kind of activity than cursing. During the struggle for civil rights in the USA, many Christians engaged in pastoral rebuke with the managers of restaurants which refused to serve black people, telling them that what they were doing was contrary to the word of God and was poisoning their own souls. A similar strong stand was taken by certain South African Christians against apartheid. More recent examples of the exercise of this kind of ministry include vigils organised by churches outside massage parlours and sex shops, boycotts of products made by companies involved in exploitative practices or using slave labour, and the women's peace camp at the gates of the Faslane nuclear submarine base.

This is a difficult and highly divisive area. Activities which some Christians might want to curse – gay marriages, for example – others would want to bless. The militant opposition to abortion on the part of certain Christian groups, which certainly falls into the category of cursing, leaves other Christians feeling very uneasy. There is considerable debate within contemporary Christianity about the desirability of the notion of spiritual warfare and the attitude of movements like the March for Jesus, which seek to go into what its participants regard as demonised areas and redeem them for Christ. I suspect that, were they return today, the Celtic saints would be on the side of the spiritual warriors. The whole enterprise of redemption was central to their ministry. Columba's action in turning a poisoned well into a healing spring by blessing the water and drinking from it perhaps finds a modern parallel in Christians establishing a presence in a red-light area and working with the prostitutes in an effort to change the culture of crime and exploitation. If their biographers are to be believed, the Celtic saints confronted head on the pagan priests and wizards and the evil forces of their day. Today, having largely banished 'Onward, Christian soldiers', 'Rise up, O men of God' and 'Soldiers of Christ arise' in our desperate desire to be politically correct and avoid sexist or militarist language, we have become

altogether too timid and lily-livered about confronting evil.

If we perhaps need to be more robust in our cursing, we could certainly do with taking the whole
business of blessing much more seriously. In our
sophisticated and secularised culture benediction has
lost its central place and been largely relegated even
in Christian circles to a brief and sometimes rather
perfunctory dismissal at the end of the Sunday service. If we encountered people going round blessing
every person they met and every home they entered,
we would probably think them slightly deranged. Yet
this is exactly what many priests, pastors and ministers in other less sophisticated and supposedly more
primitive Christian cultures still do. I remember
being struck some years ago by a visiting African
priest who blessed with a broad grin everyone whom
he met and every home he went into. He was very
much in the tradition of Columba. In this as in other
respects contemporary African churches are perhaps
much closer to the spirit of Celtic Christianity than
those in the British Isles. There are British Christians
who dispense blessings liberally and unselfcon-
sciously today, notably in my experience members of
the Salvation Army, but most of us are inhibited in
this area. We would do well to take our cue from our
African brothers and sisters and our Celtic (and
Jewish) ancestors and develop a ministry of benediction.

We live in a society where many people are crying

out for blessing, healing and affirmation because they are frightened, lonely, depressed, lacking in self-esteem or just stressed out. How badly we need a new set of beatitudes: 'Blessed are the carers, the redundant, the depressives'. Good pastoral care starts with a sense of benediction, of speaking well of the individual, whatever his or her status. At a rather different level, not without its own pastoral dimension, there is a growing call for and provision of church services involving the blessing of second marriages, long-term same-sex relationships and even pets and animals, and restoring traditional and latterly often neglected occasions for blessing in the agricultural year such as Rogation and Lammas. It is good that churches are responding to this growing demand for liturgical benediction, much of which comes from the great unchurched majority, and rediscovering both the will and the skill to bless outside the confines of that brief prayer at the end of public worship which has all too often become a mere formality rushed through as if to say 'Well, that's the end of that, thank goodness' rather than being a real discharge of love and power.[20]

It is good to find the ministry of blessing being exercised in an imaginative way by many clergy. A recent example which gained considerable publicity involved a Hertfordshire vicar sprinkling holy water over a lollipop lady in a ceremony to bless a road crossing used by primary school pupils. Alan Horsley, Vicar of St Peter's, Rickmansworth, carried out the blessing at the end of a special road-safety day for pupils and at the request of the school's headteacher who was concerned that children were not using the official crossing supervised by the lollipop lady but crossing on a more dangerous section of road. In a nice blend of liturgical benediction and practical road-safety training, five children, dressed in cassocks and carrying a cross, the holy water and incense, led the rest of the school out on to the crossing for the ceremony of blessing. In another recent initiative on a much larger scale Nigel McCulloch, the Bishop of Wakefield, personally blessed 20,000 people during the course of 1999 as part of the diocese's preparations for the millennium. The blessing given to each of those who knelt before him was very simple – 'The Lord bless you, that you may take the light of Christ into the new millennium' – but by all accounts had a profound influence on many who received it.

The recovery of blessing both within church worship and beyond it in a whole range of different contexts has been a notable feature of the current Celtic Christian revival. Celtic and Celtic-style blessings are being increasingly used in services, especially those which involve rites of passage and have a strong pastoral dimension such as baptisms, weddings and funerals. George Coppen, Vicar of Kidlington, near Oxford, makes considerable use in funerals both of the traditional Irish blessing 'May the road rise to meet you', and of adaptations of blessings from the *Carmina*:

God, bless to us the pathway on which you go,
God, bless the earth that is beneath your sole;
Bless, O God, and give to him your love,
O God of gods, bless his rest and his repose;
Bless, O God, and give to him your love,
And bless, O God of gods, his repose.

It is sometimes said that the proliferation of blessings in the *Carmina* was a direct consequence of the shortage of priests in the Western Isles in the late nineteenth century. They represented a kind of lay liturgy which could be used in the absence of professional clerical prayers. The ministry of blessing can surely be carried out as effectively by lay people as those who are ordained. Indeed, it can often take place within the context of a family or household. The Community of Aidan and Hilda encourages members to bless their homes, echoing a practice followed in the Iona Community where common rooms and kitchens are blessed at the beginning and end of each season. Ray Simpson has provided a series of 'Celtic Blessings for Everyday Life' which cover computers ('I programme my computer with the love of God'), exams ('I bless this exam in the name of the Designer of Truth'), parties, pets and cars ('May it bless the earth it will travel on') and all kinds of life situations from leaving school and a girl's first period to divorce, redundancy and mid-life crisis.[21]

It is, of course, the case that blessing comes more naturally to some people than to others. It is in part a gift, in part a skill and in part a matter of being in tune with God and the rhythms of his creation. In pre-Christian Celtic religion there was a strong belief that everyone could come into contact with the sacred and make the spiritual journey into the other world. Yet it was also recognised that certain people, the shamans or druids, through their gifts and their specialist knowledge and training, were especially open to spiritual revelation and equipped to lead others into a deeper appreciation of the sacred. So it should be in contemporary Christianity. We need to recognise that some are naturally gifted in and given to blessing and can be trained and affirmed in a ministry of benediction. This is especially important given the proven therapeutic benefits of prayer and blessing for those with mental illness.

Prayers of protection and encirclement based on the model of the Celtic *lorica* and *caim* prayers can speak powerfully to those facing depression, isolation and confusion. In *The Celtic Way* I described my own discovery, while serving as a psychiatric hospital chaplain, of the apparent therapeutic benefits of prayers such as David Adam's beautifully simple modern *caim*, 'Circle me Lord, Keep protection near and danger afar', for those suffering from depression and schizophrenia. I have since spoken and corresponded with others involved in chaplaincy work with the mentally ill and with those who have themselves been through periods of depression who have confirmed how helpful they have found both the breastplate prayers and encircling blessings. These simple, almost physical invocations of God's protective enfolding love have somehow connected when other wordier prayers have failed to have much effect.

Rediscovering the therapeutic role of blessings is an important element in the much wider development of healing ministries which has been one of the most striking trends in church life over recent decades. It would be wrong to claim that this movement takes its prime inspiration from the Celtic Christian tradition. However, there are several significant initiatives within this area which are influenced by Celtic traditions and places. At Pennant Melangell, the remote church in mid-Wales which houses the shrine of Melangell, a seventh-century virgin who sheltered a hare being hunted by a local prince, Evelyn Davies has established the Cancer Help Centre and Ministry to the Sick with the aim of enhancing the quality of the life of the very ill. It offers help and counselling, both in person and on the telephone, to those facing terminal illness and to their carers.

More broadly, we need to recover that almost unconscious vision of the Church as a community of benediction which made the Irish saints bless as a matter of course and led the Welsh praise poets to proclaim the glory of God in his created order. In this understanding, churches and Christian communities, representing the Body of Christ, are indeed colonies of heaven, speaking well of things, affirming goodness and showering blessings on a world where there is so much putting down and reductionism. As it is, churches are as full of back-biting, fault-finding, carping, criticising and bitchy gossip as any other institution, indeed often rather more so. Here is a real counter-cultural task for Christians – to celebrate and bless rather than criticise and put down. This does not preclude cursing and issuing pastoral rebukes where appropriate but it does mean all our encounters and utterances being informed by a sense of living in a redeemed and sacramental world.

Perhaps what we need above all is that leap of imagination that can look at the flower petal or the bird on the wing and see a reflection of God's grace and beauty. Celtic literature is full of poems which find the heavenly in the earthly and express the sense that every task, however humdrum, can be blessed if we see God in it. Nowhere, perhaps, is it more clearly expressed than in the familiar verses written by that great Anglo-Celt, George Herbert, in the mid-seventeenth century:

> Teach me, my God and King,
> In all things Thee to see,
> And what I do in anything
> To do it as for thee . . .

> A servant with this clause
> Makes drudgery divine:
> Who sweeps a room, as for thy laws,
> Makes that and th' action fine.

The challenge is how to make that a reality for the supermarket checkout clerk or the call-centre operator, in a culture where interpersonal contact, initiative and the exercise of imagination are being squeezed out by technology and where everything is increasingly standardised, processed and packaged. More than ever we need those who will bless, and rebuke, rather than simply chatter idly or gripe and complain, those who have the imagination and the vision to see the glory in the grey, who approach people and situations in the manner of Jesus rather than the Pharisees,

> Those who can raise
> Gold spirits of men from their rough Ape-dust,
>   and who see
> The glory, grandeur hidden in small forms:
> The planetary system in the atom, and great
>   suns
> Hid in a speck of dust. Praise we the just —
> Who are not come to judge, but bless
> Immortal things in their poor mortal dress.[22]

Penance and Pastoral Care

The single largest group of documents that have survived from the so-called golden age of Celtic Christianity are the penitentials. These depressing catalogues of punishments to fit every conceivable crime are found in considerable numbers in the manuscript collections associated with both the great Irish monasteries and the communities founded across Continental Europe by wandering Irish monks.

If the penitential rather than the Psalter, the prayer book or the volume of poetry was in fact the most ubiquitous and characteristic product of the monastic *scriptoria*, we might be excused for concluding that

Celtic Christianity had an unhealthy fixation on penance and punishment, an obsessive concern with the most trivial sins and a Pelagian view that overemphasised the importance of human effort and behaviour and left little room for the workings of God's free and prevenient grace.

In fact, however, closer examination of the penitentials, and particularly of the context in which they were used, reveals a remarkably sensitive approach to pastoral care based on an overwhelming sense of the power of forgiveness and the need to aid the growth and development of the human personality. Several recent studies have pointed to both the pastoral value and the innovative nature of the penitential system developed in the Irish monasteries between the seventh and tenth centuries. In his contribution to *Pastoral Care before the Parish*, which focuses on the pastoral role of the Church in the early Irish laws, Thomas Charles-Edwards points out that while

> it may be true that the penitentials make rather
> depressing reading, yet their desire to prescribe
> a penance for each and every shameful deed is
> only a consequence of the wish to show that
> no sin is so terrible and despicable that it is
> beyond the mercy of God and the redemptive
> power of Christian penance.[1]

J. T. McNeill argues in his classic *History of the Cure of Souls* that the Celtic church made a major and distinctive contribution to the development of pastoral care by developing the concept of confession, penance and spiritual direction.[2] Hugh Connolly, an Irish priest who has written a fascinating book on the Irish penitentials and their relevance today, suggests that the Irish monastic church possessed 'an extraordinarily lucid insight into the mystery of divine forgiveness'.[3]

In the early Church, sin and guilt had been largely dealt with through a mechanism of public confession and penance. Those held to be sinners, or who felt themselves full of guilt, were brought before the local bishop and subjected to public humiliation and punishment, often in the presence of elders or members of their own congregation. The system of penance which the Irish monasteries are generally credited with introducing, and which was to spread through the whole Church in the Middle Ages, was very different, being an essentially private process of repeated confession made by the penitent to a confessor or spiritual director. The penitentials were an essential feature of this new approach, being produced as manuals for use by those who heard confessions, pronounced absolution and prescribed appropriate penalties. Although they may strike us today as having a mechanical rigidity, they did, in fact, embody a more flexible approach than the old practice of non-commutable juridical penalties. In the Irish understanding, contrition and resolve to change were more important than fulfilment of legal requirement. The penance was to be accepted freely and offered to God as a sign of an inner change of heart and a true repentance rather than simply performed as a legal sentence.

The origins of this approach to penance lie in the teachings and practices of the founders of Eastern desert monasticism in fourth- and fifth-century Egypt and Syria. Probably the key figure in transmitting their ideas to the West was John Cassian, who around 415 in Marseilles founded both a monastery and a nunnery based on the principles of the desert fathers, and wrote a highly influentiual tract on the rules of Egyptian monasticism. It was in the austere, disciplined world of Irish monasticism that the principles pioneered in the Egyptian desert and promoted by Cassian were first taken up on a significant scale in the West. At the heart of the Irish penitential system lay the monks' desire to be martyrs, expressing their faithful and costly witness to Christ by dying daily with him and subjecting themselves to a punishing self-sacrificial regime which included fasting, doing without sleep, immersions in cold water, frequent genuflections and long periods with arms outstretched in the cross vigil.

The theological thinking which underpinned these penitential practices was emphatically not a doctrine of salvation by works. It was rather a sense of the costly discipline and self-sacrifice involved in being a disciple of Christ. There was also an understanding of the healing power of the penitential disciplines not just in terms of acknowledging and coming to terms with one's own failings but in moving on from them to the new life and growth which springs from a sense of forgiveness. In Connolly's words, 'it was not as though one somehow earned forgiveness through penitential activity; rather, in the practice of therapeutic sacrifice one re-discovered in one's heart God's call to forgiveness.'[4]

The Irish penitentials were designed to promote personal growth and development as much as to punish and correct. They prescribed penances for the eight chief vices: gluttony (which covered excessive talking as well as excessive eating and drinking), fornication, avarice (which was taken to include a general lack of regard for others and selfishness), anger, dejection, languor, vainglory and pride, as well as for a host of other lesser offences. Following Cassian, the principle on which they operated was that of *contraria contrariis sanantur*, contraries are cured by their contraries. Thus the person who has displayed anger has to cultivate meekness, the one who has been guilty of avarice must exercise generosity and the dejected should strive after spiritual joy. In this way, the penitentials did not provide simply punishments that fitted the crime, but carefully calculated programmes to change attitudes and behaviour. The negative element must be replaced by a positive one as part of a progression away from sin and towards Christian perfection. As the Penitential of Finnian put it, 'By contraries let us make haste to cure contraries and to cleanse away these faults from our hearts and introduce heavenly virtues in their place.'[5]

At the heart of the Irish penitential system was the practice of regular private confession and absolution, understood not as a mechanical ritual but as a genuine expression of repentance and desire for *metanoia* or change. The penance set by the confessor was seen in similar terms, not as a mere punishment but rather as an earnest of repentance and an aid to spiritual and moral growth. Confession was regarded as being a necessary part of the daily routine: 'As the floor is swept each day so is the soul cleansed every day by confession'.[6] Routine and regular as it should be, however, confession was not to be undertaken lightly or in a casual manner. It should involve a serious confrontation with the state of one's soul and a penetrating and honest examination of the individual conscience. This was one of the main reasons why under the influence of the Irish monastic system, *confessio*, as what had previously been called penance was increasingly known, became a private rather than a public matter.

More than this, confession became a whole state of mind, not in the sense of our modern prurient obsession with kiss-and-tell stories and television programmes exposing people's long-held secrets, but rather in terms of a temperament of openness, humility and honesty. It is no accident that one of the seminal texts of Celtic Christianity, the spiritual autobiography of Patrick, is entitled *Confessio* and begins with the words 'I Patrick, a sinner, the rudest and least of all the faithful and most contemptible to many'. This sense of self-abasement is not a grovelling creepiness of the Uriah Heep kind, nor a false modesty. It reflects genuine Christian humility, the poverty in spirit commended in the Beatitudes. The sense of unworthiness and vulnerability that pervades Patrick's *Confessio* is as much the authentic voice of Celtic Christianity as the tales of super-human wonder-workers which fill the pages of the later lives of the saints. A similar attitude pervades the writings of the desert fathers, as Benedicta Ward points out:

> The monk is involved with mankind in the
> deepest sense, and where, by penance and
> prayer and self-loss, he learns to stand before
> God in a 'life-time's death of love'. One part of
> torn and broken humanity is placed before its
> Saviour. When the monk defines himself, it is
> as a sinner, a weak man, not a strong one, not
> as one 'by whom the world is kept in being'.[7]

This sense of human weakness underlay the penitential sytem. With its severe regime of punish-ments, vigils and fasts, it doubtless strikes many in our comfortable and indulgent age as altogether too strict and self-denying. Yet it recognised the human capacity to slip back and the need for constant encouragement and stimulation to aid self-growth and development. The Irish penitentials replaced an essentially static approach to sin and guilt with a dynamic one based on the model and principle of pilgrimage. Penance became a process of repeated confession and absolution during the individual's journey from cradle to grave. In Hugh Connolly's words:

> The symbols of Celtic Christianity, whilst at times harsh and severe, had the merit of reminding each Christian that they had to make their own journey. Thus, life was focussed, life was purposed. In journeying toward Christ, Christians also journeyed deeper into themselves and began to forge their personal moral identity. They lived with the possibility of sin; but they also had a remedy for sin, and after each fall arose stronger and better equipped to forge a new moral life.
>
> The Celtic Christian, moreover, started from a keen awareness of his capacity for sin. His humility was not some exaggerated form of self-abasement, but rather stemmed from a consciousness of what it means to be human, to be in need. For that reason, the Christian journey, and *ergo* the moral journey, was never something to be made alone, but something to be undertaken in the company of those who

understood and appreciated the struggles of the human situation.[8]

Although private, the regular act of confession and absolution which stood at the heart of the Irish penitential system was not a solitary affair. It was rather a meeting of souls in which the confessor or spiritual director accompanied and led the penitent on his or her journey. This was essentially a pastoral relationship which was understood in the context of a ministry of healing. Indeed, those dispensing the *medicamenta penitentiae*, as they were often called, were frequently described as physicians of the soul. Such language was not, of course, peculiar to Celtic Christianity. The understanding of priests as doctors charged with the cure of souls is a key theme of the famous treatise on pastoral care written by Gregory the Great at the end of the sixth century. It was, however, particularly marked in the Irish penitentials. A penitential attributed to Columbanus, for example, makes an explicit comparison between medical doctors and those responsible for the cure of souls:

> For as doctors of the body compound their medicines in diverse kinds; thus they heal wounds in one manner, sicknesses in another, boils in another, eye diseases in another, fractures in another, burns in another. So also should spiritual doctors treat with diverse kinds of cures the wounds of souls, their sicknesses (offences), pains, ailments and infirmities.[9]

Although the penitential system had its origins in the particular rigours and disciplines of the monastic life, it did not just apply to monks or priests. The penitentials make clear that the *medicamenta penitentiae* were also dispensed to the laity. Different penances were prescribed depending on whether the offender was a cleric or layman. The late-sixth-century *Paenitentiale Vinniani*, attributed to Finnian of Moville, and possibly the earliest extant Irish penitential, notes with regard to those who have plotted to strike or kill their neighbours, 'if a cleric he shall do penance for half a year . . . but if he is a layman he shall do penance for seven days; since he is a man of this world, his guilt is lighter in this world and his reward less in the world to come.'[10] According to their biographers, several of the Celtic saints were regarded as outstanding pastors and attracted numerous penitents seeking relief from burdens of sin and guilt. Jonas' *Life* of Columbanus notes that 'the people flocked together from all sides for the medicine of penance'.[11] Many of the lay people found in Irish monasteries were penitents who often spent considerable periods serving out penances within the monastic communities. Several monastic *familiae* developed remote communities specifically for penitents, as Columba did at Mag Luinge on Tiree where he regularly sent people for periods of up to seven years.

The *medicamenta penitentiae* were part of an extensive ministry of pastoral care and counselling which was exercised in the Irish monasteries and their offshoots in mainland Britain. Adamnan portrays Columba as undertaking an extensive pastoral ministry on Iona and provides several telling examples of his counselling skills. There is the story of the wife who comes to him because she can no longer face sleeping with her ugly husband. She hopes that Columba will tell her to cross the sea and join a women's monastery but in fact he gets her and her husband to fast with him for a day. As they sleep the following evening, he prays for them and the next day the woman awakes transformed – 'The husband whom I hated I love today. My heart was changed from loathing to love.'[12] Several other stories indicate Columba's abilities to reconcile people both to themselves and to others from whom they have become distant or estranged. This pastoral gift is often shown being exercised through the medium of penance. Many of those who visited Iona came as penitents, seeking to atone for some crime or to come to terms with feelings of guilt and remorse.

The dispensing of penance often went hand in hand with an insistence on restitution and reparation for harm inflicted on others. Another of Adamnan's stories concerns an Irishman who had killed a man in his native Connaught and made the long journey to Iona to 'wipe out his sins on a pilgrimage'. Columba told him that he must spend seven years on Tiree. At the end of that period, he returned to Iona to be told by the saint that he must now go back to the relative who, in return for a promise of servitude for life, had paid the ransom due if he was not to suffer death for his crime, and from whom he had escaped. Columba even gave the man a decorated sword to give to his deserted master as a peace offering and told him to discharge his debt to his estranged family. This was done and the penitent returned to Iona, took his monastic vows and served for many years as a monk at Mag Luinge where he worked gathering reeds in the reed-bed.[13] The *Penitential* of Columbanus lays down that 'if any of the laity has shed blood in a brawl, or wounded his neighbour, let him be compelled to restore all the damage he has done; but if he has nothing to pay with, let him first attend to his neighbour's work while he is sick.' It also requires any layman who has stolen his neighbour's ox or ass to 'restore to his neighbour the loss which he has caused before doing penance for three forty-day periods on bread and water.[14] Other penitentials similarly promote the principle of restorative justice, emphasising the importance of offenders meeting their victims and making reparation for their crimes.

Another essentially pastoral role fulfilled by Celtic monks was that of counsellor and prophet. A third of Adamnan's life of Columba is made up of stories testifying to the saint's prophetic powers and providing examples of his gifts in telepathy, thought transference, clairvoyance and precognition. At one level these traits, which are attributed to other Celtic saints, can be seen as a Christianised version of the soothsaying skills of the Irish druids and bards. There is also, of course, a strong biblical basis for these kinds of activity in the Old Testament stories of figures who can interpret God's intentions for the future as they are revealed in dreams and in Paul's identification of prophecy as a gift of the Spirit. While many of Columba's prophecies seem simply to demonstrate his prodigious gifts as a seer, leading one recent author to describe him as 'the father of second sight', others clearly come within the context of what would now be called a counselling relationship.[15] Like other leading Celtic churchmen, he acted as confidant and adviser to kings and noblemen, as well as to a host of lesser mortals who sought his counsel and valued his skills of discernment. Doubtless this role often involved pointing out to people the consequences of their actions and telling them what would happen if they followed a particular course. It is not too fanciful to suggest that Iona in the sixth century exerted something of the same pull as Delphi had a thousand years earlier. Crowds who flocked there to consult the oracle were doubtless motivated by the same mixture of curiosity and deep pastoral need.

It was not just Celtic monasteries which served as centres of pastoral care in the centuries before the development of a settled parish system in the British Isles. The Anglo-Saxon minsters also took on this role, their teams of clergy going out into the surrounding community like the Celtic monks to baptise, catechise, administer the sacraments and bury the dead. One of their most important tasks was the visitation of the seriously ill and dying. This ministry was understood very much as an aspect of the *cura animarum*, with the emphasis being put firmly on spiritual rather than physical healing. A seventh-century commentary on the Epistle of James, which contains the earliest known Irish reference to the practice of anointing the sick, defines sickness as *infirmitas peccati* (the infirmity of sin) and portrays the oil used in anointing as a sign of God's merciful forgiveness. A ritual for visiting the sick which probably dates from the eleventh century is found inscribed on one of the pages of the Book of Deer and was almost certainly used by monks engaged in pastoral work in the north-east of Scotland. It includes a brief rite of communion, or *viaticum*, in which the sick are offered food for their journey into the next world. As in the earlier Irish source, the emphasis is very much on the spiritual goal of eternal salvation rather than on physical healing.[16]

One striking aspect of the pastoral care offered both inside and outside the Irish monasteries does seem to have been distinctively Celtic. This was the figure of the soul friend, or *anamchara*, who played a key role in the penitential system. It was to his soul friend that the monk, and possibly the layman too, went to make his confession and receive absolution, the appropriate *medicamenta penitentiae* and doubtless confidential counselling as well. There are tantalisingly few references to this particular feature of monastic life although it seems that every monk had a soul friend who acted as confessor and spiritual director. One of the most intriguing, and often quoted mentions of the soul-friend system is given as part of the entry for 1 February, the feast day of Brigit, in the Martyrology of Oengus:

> A young cleric of the community of Ferns, a fosterling of Brigit's, comes to her with dainties. He was with her in the refectory consuming his ration. Once upon a time then, after going to communion, Brigit strikes a clapper. 'Well, thou young cleric there, hast thou a soulfriend?' 'I have, indeed' says the young cleric. 'Let us sing his requiem.' 'Why so?' asks the young cleric. 'He has died' says Brigit. 'When thou hadst finished half thy ration I saw that he was dead.' 'How knewest thou that?' 'Easy to say: from the time that thy soulfriend was dead I saw that thy ration was put into thy trunk, thou being quite headless. Go forth: eat nothing till thou gettest a soul-friend, for a man without a soulfriend is a body without a head: for it is water of a limy lough, neither good for drinking nor washing, that is like a man without a soulfriend.'[17]

Soul-friendship has obvious biblical roots in the relationships that existed between David and

Jonathan, Barnabas and Saul, and Paul and Timothy. Like so much else, the Irish monks almost certainly took it up in imitation of a practice pioneered by the desert fathers who despite their quest for solitude often shared their cells with a *syncellus* (cell-mate) who acted as both close friend and spiritual guide. While living in a monastery at Bethlehem, John Cassian, who did so much to spread the principles of desert monasticism in Europe, had shared his cell with another monk called Germanus. Given that the cell was where the monk encountered God, the *syncellus* relationship was particularly deep and intimate. To share one's cell with another was to share one's innermost self and secrets. The desert fathers called it *exagoreusis*, opening one's heart to another. It is reflected in the scene, depicted on several Irish high crosses, of the desert hermits Paul of Thebes and Antony sitting together under a palm tree.

It is difficult to determine to what extent the figure of the *anamchara* was found outside the bounds of the monastic *vallum*. We know that kings and nobles had soul friends, who seem always to have been clergy, but there is little evidence as to how widespread the practice was lower down the social scale, nor is it really clear whether only monks and priests could act as soul friends. That lay people had soul friends, and that the system could be abused, is evident from an eighth-century Hiberno-Latin text which notes that 'laymen fancy that in order to get to heaven it is enough to give something to their soul friends and that their soul friends will thenceforth be at their command'.[18] The *Riagail Phatraic* (Rule of Patrick), an old Irish text dealing with the proper behaviour of clergy, lays down that the bishop should be the soul friend of nobles and heads of churches and those in orders. As we have already noted, monks often acted as advisers and counsellors to kings, much as the druids and filid had in pre-Christian days, and were also more widely consulted as holy men. This general counselling role, however, was probably rather different from the more intimate one-to-one relationship of the *anamchara*, certainly as it operated in the monastic context. It is difficult to determine the boundaries between soul-friendship on the *syncellus* model and the guru/prophet/counsellor role undertaken by many Celtic monks. What is clear is the high value that was placed both inside and outside religious communities on spiritual direction and guidance: 'To go to a devout sage is good, to direct one's path. A devout sage to guide you, it is good to avoid punishment. Although you consider yourself very strong, be not your own guide.'[19]

Particular value was put on soul friends being present to one another at death. When Columba intuited that his soul friend and fellow monk Cailton would not live long, he sent a message inviting him to come to Iona 'for, loving you as a friend, I want you to end your days with me here'.[20] A touching story relates how when Ciaran of Clonmacnoise was dying, he waited in his little chapel for his soul friend Kevin of Glendalough to come and be with him. Although he died before Kevin arrived,

> Ciaran's spirit returned from heaven and re-
> entered his body so that he could commune
> with Kevin and welcome him. The two friends
> stayed together from the one watch to another,
> engaged in mutual conversation, and strength-
> ened their friendship. Then Ciaran blessed
> Kevin, and Kevin blessed water and adminis-
> tered the Eucharist to Ciaran. Ciaran gave his
> bell to Kevin as a sign of their lasting unity.[21]

In the Hebridean islands, and possibly in other places as well, the role of the soul friend seems to have developed into a highly specialist form of lay ministry to the dying. In his notes for Marjory Kennedy-Fraser's classic *Songs of the Hebrides*, published in 1909, the minister and Gaelic folklorist Kenneth MacLeod, who himself came from the island of Eigg, noted that

> in the days of the old Celtic church, the
> Death-croon was chanted over the dying by
> the *anam-chara*, the soul friend, assisted by three
> chanters. Later on, the rite passed into the
> hands of *seanairean a'bhaile*, the elders of the
> township, and the *mnathan-tuiridh*, the mourning
> women, the latter developing into a profes-
> sional class, whose services could always be
> obtained for a consideration.[22]

Alexander Carmichael gives a particularly moving description of Hebridean death blessings in his notes to the *Carmina Gadelica*. His words suggest that the figure of the *anamchara* was still in existence in the Hebrides in the late nineteenth century and specifically associated with this practice:

> Death blessings vary in words but not in spirit. These death blessings are known by various names, such as: *Beannachadh Bais* (Death Blessing), *Treoraich Anama* (Soul Leading), *Fois Anama* (Soul Peace), and other names familiar to the people.
>
> The soul peace is intoned, not necessarily by a cleric, over the dying, and the man or the woman who says it is called *anam-chara* (soul friend). He or she is held in special affection by the friends of the dying person ever after. The soul peace is slowly sung – all present earnestly joining the soul friend in beseeching the Three Persons of the Godhead and all the saints of heaven to receive the departing soul of earth. During the prayer the soul friend makes the sign of the cross with the right thumb over the lips of the dying.[23]

Carmichael noted that the death blessings and soul leadings were pronounced by the *anamchara* with the purpose of speeding the dying person on his or her pilgrimage, which was variously described as being across *abhuinn dubh a bhais* (the black river of death), *cuan mor na duibhre* (the great ocean of darkness), or *beanntaibh na bith-bhuantachd* (the mountains of eternity). At the moment of death, when 'the soul is seen ascending like a bright ball of light into the clouds', those present would join the *anamchara* in saying:

> The poor soul is now set free
> Outside the soul-shrine;
> O kindly Christ of the free blessings.
> Encompass Thou my love in time.[24]

Soul friendship has been one of the most popular themes in the current revival of enthusiasm for Celtic Christianity. One of the first people to take it up was the Anglican priest Kenneth Leech whose *Soul Friend: A Study in Spirituality*, first published in 1977, persuasively argued for a contemporary theology of spiritual direction based on the model of the soul friend and on the quality of discernment which enables individuals to move towards freedom. In a more direct imitation of Irish monastic practice, those joining the Community of Aidan and Hilda are allocated a soul friend who accompanies them on their first journey in the coracle and throughout their subsequent pilgrimage of faith. This may well echo the procedures adopted in the early Irish church with respect to newcomers to the faith. The life of Colman speaks of children being baptised, later confirmed and after seven years being taken to a soul friend with whom they read the Psalms and hymns.

The principle of one-to-one guidance and support has, of course, been long used in a variety of pastoral situations. It has been very successfully employed in self-help groups like Alcoholics Anonymous and underlies the Stephen ministry programme now pursued by many churches in the United States whereby lay church members are trained to counsel and support those facing difficulties. More recently the notion of mentoring, which is in some ways very similar to soul-friending, has been widely taken up in the commercial world. David Clutterbuck's book, *Everyone Needs a Mentor*, published by the Institute of Personnel Management in 1990, argues that employees assigned a mentor develop a sense of self-worth, learn about the values and ways of a company and gain insight into management process. Many of the new house churches and fellowships have developed systems of spiritual mentoring or shepherding, although these have sometimes become rather heavy-handed and authoritarian. Perhaps a feature of the Irish *anamchara* model is relevant here. Although the soul friend could be directive and challenging, he was never to be judgemental. Some sound advice for mentors is contained in an eighth-century rule for soul friends: 'You do well to correct. You do not do well to reprove. The mind rebels against reproof. It is humble at being corrected.'[25]

We need to re-emphasise the value of soul-friendship at a time when pastoral care is increasingly being conceived of as a task for professional or semi-professional counsellors trained in various branches of psychotherapy. Several voices have recently and rightly questioned whether Christian pastoral care and counselling is losing its distinctive spiritual focus and being subsumed in an essentially secular movement.[26] Developing the qualities of discernment and guidance found in the *anamchara* would enable and equip Christians to take on a variety of counselling and mentoring roles on a one-to-one basis. The practicalities of soul-friending today are well explored in Ray Simpson's excellent book, *Soul-Friendship: Celtic Insights into Spiritual Mentoring* (1999). He is much attracted to the Celtic model of the soul friend as the companion on a journey of discovery: 'Both soul friend and seeker are on the journey though the soul friend has been journeying longer, or has been given grace to travel further.'[27] As well as surveying the historic roots and principles of soul-friendship, Simpson provides a highly practical 'beginner's guide' to finding and becoming a soul friend. He suggests a role for religious communities in the training of soul friends and proposes that they be commissioned by their local church for this work.

There is perhaps a wider and more basic need to affirm simple friendship as a Christian vocation. It is a declining commodity in our society thanks to a combination of ever-increasing pressures on people's time, the trend towards more privatised and individualised lifestyles, and the breakdown of bonds of trust and affection in families and communities. More and more people are isolated, and at the same time there seem to be fewer and fewer people with the time and the ability simply to sit and listen. There is a whole theology of friendship to be explored and promoted. It is beautifully expressed in Ecclesiasticus 6.14-16 (REB):

A faithful friend is a secure shelter;
whoever finds one, finds a treasure.
A faithful friend is beyond price;
there is no measure of his worth.
A faithful friend is an elixir of life,
found only by those who fear the Lord.

In its availability and vulnerability friendship of any really meaningful kind is a costly rather than an easy option. The absence of close friends pushes many towards the brink of depression or sends them into the arms of counsellors and doctors. One of the groups most in need of this kind of friendship are clergy, who are often desperately isolated and unable to share their deepest feelings and fears with anyone. Another group are members of the medical profession. Perhaps we should start close to home and make sure that every minister and doctor has a soul friend and can experience what is so well expressed by George Eliot:

Oh the comfort, the inexpressible comfort of
feeling safe with a person; having neither to
weigh thoughts nor measure words, but to
pour them all out, just as they are, chaff and
grain together, knowing that a faithful hand
will take and sift them, keep what is worth
keeping, and then, with the breath of kindness,
blow the rest away.[28]

It would also be good to recover the role of the *anamchara* in the care of the terminally ill and dying. In my
experience one of the most effective examples of
soul-friendship in contemporary pastoral care has
been the development of the 'buddy' system among
those suffering from HIV/Aids. Those in the terminal
stages of this terrible illness are given a 'buddy' who
acts as soul-mate, companion and practical helper.
Recent decades have seen enormous strides in the
spiritual as well as physical care of the dying through
the development of the hospice movement and
Macmillan nurses. Too often, however, people face
their final illnesses with no soul friend to prepare
them for their coming pilgrimage. We need to
encourage and train individuals, including ideally
those working in hospitals and nursing homes, who
can offer appropriate contemporary death blessings
and soul leadings. We also desperately need prayers
for the dying which pick up the pilgrimage theme
and prepare souls for their journey out of this world
and into the next. Such prayers are as important in

both pastoral and spiritual terms for the living as for the dying. As Penelope Wilcock has rightly observed:

> To accompany other people, along with their loved ones, up to the gate of death is to enter Holy Ground. To stand in an awesome place where the wind of the Spirit blows; to encounter peace and grief, insight, intimacy and pain on a level not found in ordinary living. By the side of the dying we learn stillness, waiting, simply being; the arts of quietness and keeping watch, prayer beyond words.[29]

There is another pastoral task fulfilled by soul friends and more generally by Celtic monks which perhaps needs to be taken on by the Church today. I am thinking of their role as prophets, seers, guides and counsellors. Many of those who sought out Columba no doubt came as much for his gifts of discernment and his counselling skills as for his ability to see into the future. Today more and more people are going to fortune-tellers, reading runes and tarot cards and consulting astrologers and horoscopes. I suspect that many of them too are looking for guidance and advice as much as clairvoyance. The Church should engage with these people's needs. I am not suggesting that ministers and priests acquire crystal balls and gaze into the future, but it is important that we try to meet these seekers where they are with open-ended counselling and guidance. Otherwise we leave them prey to all kinds of charlatans and unhealthy influences.

At a time when the so-called New Age movement is reviving or reconstructing many of the beliefs and practices associated with pagan and pre-Christian cultures, it is instructive to recall how Celtic Christian soul friends took over the roles of the shamans in seventh- and eighth-century Britain and Ireland. In Ray Simpson's words:

> Christian Celts rejected the use of psychic forces to control others and the practice of shamanism, but they believed that God as revealed in Christ could use them to shape people's lives by freeing them from fear and other evils. They renounced the use of magic, drugs and spiritism, but Christian soul friends sought to be people whom the population would feel able to consult as much as they consulted the shamans. They gave up the shape-shifting that shamans went into trances to achieve, yet they did not give up the idea of shaping people according to their true image of God.[30]

We could do with recovering this shamanic aspect of Celtic Christian soul-friendship and pastoral care today. It means more attention being paid, in both ministerial and lay training, to spiritual guidance and direction and fostering qualities of discernment. It also means more contemporary Christians being trained in and open to techniques of relaxation and spiritual guidance which are nowadays often associated with Eastern religions rather than with Christianity – transcendental meditation, for example, which as Adrian Smith, a Roman Catholic missionary priest, and others have demonstrated is quite compatible with Christian belief and practice despite its origins in the Vedic tradition of Hinduism and its New Age connotations.[31] There is, in fact, an increasing openness on the part of many Christians to holistic healing and 'alternative' therapies and techniques. There is also a growing interest in exorcism and deliverance ministry. This latter area needs to be approached with caution and in co-operation with psychiatrists and medical practitioners. There is no doubt, however, that sensitively practised by those with appropriate training and back-up, exorcism, spiritual healing and driving out demons through prayer and laying on of hands can be therapeutic for those who feel themselves to be possessed by evil spirits. A recent report by the Health Education Authority, *Promoting Mental Health, The Role of Faith Communities*, urges doctors and psychiatrists not to dismiss spiritual therapies and prayer even if they lack a scientific basis.

The Celtic models of soul friend, seer and even shaman may have considerable relevance in contemporary Christian pastoral care, but surely there can be no room nowadays for the approach exemplified by the Irish penitentials? Their obsession with petty failings and providing precise punishments for every conceivable crime seems oppressively legalistic and to spring from a psychological outlook that we would now classify as repressed, if not deranged. Yet the fundamental theme that underlay the penitential system, the central importance of confession, rightly understood and practised, to spiritual and psychological health, is one that we badly need to recover.

Confession has an extraordinarily prominent place in our media-saturated secular culture. It forms the subject matter for our most popular daytime television shows, hosted by Oprah Winfrey, Jerry Springer and Robert Kilroy-Silk, in which people bare their souls and speak to audiences of millions about the intimate details of their private lives. It is highly doubtful if this form of public confession is in any way therapeutic – it operates entirely at the level of entertainment, and at a pretty low level, which panders to the worst instincts of voyeurism and prurience. It makes a travesty of the fundamental human need to get things off our chests, release long pent-up and damaging feelings of guilt and make a fresh start unburdened by past failures. I have to say that I do not think the way we handle confession in church is much better. In some traditions a rather generalised prayer of confession is gabbled through by the congregation near the beginning of the service, in others it is spoken by the minister or worship leader alone on behalf of all. This is either

followed by a brief word of absolution from the
minister or priest or simply left hanging in the air.
The whole process tends to be very formulaic, very
predictable and very superficial. Where the words of
confession are made more specific and focused, they
can be highly inappropriate – as when a congregation made up largely of elderly widows and spinsters
of impeccable moral character finds itself confessing
to carnal lusts.

The element of confession in public worship,
which for most Protestants at least is probably the
only occasion when they engage in *confessio*, woefully
fails to address the Christian requirement, and the
fundamental human need, to confront our own
innermost sins, be assured of God's forgiveness and
resolve to change. It means that many, even among
that small and diminishing band who are regular
churchgoers, go through life carrying their burdens
of guilt and sin and feeling unable to wipe the slate
clean and start anew. I recall the Roman Catholic
chaplain of a hospice in Edinburgh saying how many
patients nearing the end of their lives feel a need to
unburden themselves of feelings and resentments
and obtain a great sense of release from being
forgiven with words of absolution.

As it is, especially in contemporary Protestantism,
the Church is not really providing the kind of
ministry of forgiveness and assurance and the
opportunity for progressive growth and development
which was at the heart of the Irish system of

penitentials, soul friends and regular confession. We need to recover the Celtic emphasis on continual self-examination and self-awareness, on genuine repentance and resolve to change and on confession located in the context of ongoing spiritual direction and a lifelong process of growth and development. I suspect that we also need to recover the personal, one-to-one dimension of Celtic *confessio*. Protestants have been rightly suspicious of the mechanical, formulaic character of the traditional Roman Catholic sacrament of confession. Many Roman Catholic churches have now discarded their dark and sinister confessional boxes and replaced them with a much more open face-to-face, or even side-by-side, dialogue as the central feature of what is now called the sacrament of reconciliation. Protestant churches would do well to follow suit and develop as part of their own pastoral ministries one-to-one sessions with trained soul friends and counsellors. Perhaps reconciliation is a better word than confession to describe the underlying dynamic and the looked-for outcome of these encounters. We should not, however, neglect the element of *metanoia*, personal conversion and change, implicit in the term confession, nor the element of forgiveness and absolution which also goes with it. It should indeed be a highly positive liberating experience, rather than the negative one it is so often portrayed as, and indeed so often is. As Hugh Connolly notes in his reflection on the Celtic model:

Confession is not merely a verbal recital of
one's faults but a revelation of a changed inner
attitude to God and to one's fellow men and
women. And the fact that this exercise is carried out before God and his minister is itself
an act of faith and worship by which God is
praised, his justice acknowledged and his
mercy proclaimed.

Confession, then, is another stage in that
process whereby, as Columbanus would say,
Christ is allowed to replace the image of the
sinful despot within us with his own holy
image. This, in turn, calls the penitent toward a
renewed commitment to confess Christ before
others in his daily life. Confession brings about
an interior freedom in which the repentant
sinner becomes capable of living out his
Christian response once more. As Columbanus
explains in his pentitential, by this process 'the
heart is healed and becomes a stranger to
offence and envy'.[32]

Regular confession should figure more prominently in Christian programmes of pastoral care and
counselling as well as in spiritual direction. These
have been rightly criticised for conforming too much
to current secular psychological fads, being too self-
centred and not sufficiently anchored in the Christian
emphasis on repentance and *metanoia*. R. A.
Lambourne's critique of the pastoral counselling

movement of the 1960s along these lines has been echoed by recent writers like Paul Goodliff, Francis Bridger and David Atkinson.[33] Kenneth Leech devoted a thirty-page appendix at the end of his book, *Soul Friend*, to the subject of spiritual direction and the sacrament of reconciliation, in which he argued that confession and forgiveness are at the heart of spiritual direction, and commended a system of regular private confession, more informal than that of the traditional church confessional but not without its ritual and liturgical elements.

Other aspects of the Irish penitential system are also rightly coming back into favour today especially in the field of penal policy. The principle of curing by contraries to some extent underlies the growing practice of punishing anti-social behaviour, not with fines or custodial sentences, but through community service orders which enable offenders to put something back into society. The concept of restorative justice is increasingly being championed by police forces as well as victim support agencies and has recently been commended in a report on crime by the Oxford Diocesan Board for Social Responsibility. It points to a scheme run by Thames Valley Police in which first offenders are given the opportunity to meet their victims. In the words of Jo Saunders, the diocesan social responsibility officer, 'they have the chance to see each other as people, and recognise each other's vulnerability. Hopefully, an apology will result.'[34] In Aylesbury the re-offending rate among young offenders dropped from 30 to 6 per cent during 1998, apparently largely as a result of their participation in the scheme. Restorative justice is not a soft option any more than is community service. Like the acts of reparation and reconciliation which Columba demanded of the penitents who consulted him, these imaginative and apparently effective initiatives in penal policy go beyond the mere punishment of offences and seek to address deeper issues, confronting wrongdoers with the consequences of their actions and encouraging them to change direction.

Perhaps the most important message the Celtic penitential system has for us today is that the cure of damaged and disordered souls is not a matter of simple once-for-all remedies but a process of continual call to repentance and self-awareness, assurance of forgiveness and resolve to move on. In this ongoing process the pastor or carer, whether ordained or lay, paid professional or volunteer, walks alongside the one being given care as soul friend and fellow traveller. The Celtic model of pastor is very different from that put forward by Gregory the Great and taken up by Richard Baxter and others who have put the pastor on a pedestal and created an idealised and wholly unrealistic expectation of superhuman figures untouched by the emotions and weaknesses that beset ordinary mortals. Those expectations are bound to be cruelly shattered, as they have been spectacularly in the case of ordained clergy in all denominations as a result of well-publicised scandals often involving abuse of trust and exploitation in pastoral relationships. The note of humility and vulnerability sounded in Patrick's *Confessio* and expressed in the term *anamchara* pre-echoes the image of the wounded healer so powerfully expressed in our age by Alistair Campbell, Henri Nouwen and Jean Vanier as a key motif in Christian pastoral care.[35] This is not to deny that some are stronger than others, that there is a clear need for guidance, discernment and discipline, and that leadership and direction are important qualities in the Christian pastor. Ultimately, however, as Hugh Connolly points out, the Celtic approach to pastoral care and spiritual growth, as expressed in the penitential system, is based on the notion of a shared pilgrimage:

> All of life is seen as a form of pilgrimage. It is precisely along this life path that each Christian must make his pilgrim's progress . . .
> Recognizing that every Christian must, in some sense, experience a 'wandering in the desert' before attaining 'the promised land', it becomes apparent that he must be equipped mentally and spiritually to survive the desert ordeal . . . The penitentials are really the handbooks of the desert experience. In this model, the minister is viewed above all as fellow-traveller, fellow-pilgrim, fellow-sufferer, or to use the Celtic term, *anamchara* (soul-friend). The

emphasis in this model is predominantly one
of solidarity. Both minister and penitent are,
ultimately, pilgrims on the same pilgrim path.
The important thing is to persevere, to remain
steadfast, to stand ready and even to do battle
with the forces of evil.[36]

4

Worship

One of the questions I have been asked most often in the ten years or so that I have been writing, lecturing and preaching on Celtic Christianity is where we can find a genuine Celtic liturgy. For some enthusiasts this has almost taken on the dimensions of the quest for the Holy Grail. They are convinced that hidden away in some ruined monastic site or some dusty corner of an ancient library lies a treasure trove of ancient prayers and hymns just waiting to be discovered and made use of today.

The fact is that we have next to no liturgical texts from the 'golden age' of Celtic Christianity between the mid-fifth and mid-seventh centuries. The oldest such documents that do survive, the Antiphonary of

Bangor, a collection of hymns and prayers used in the monastery of Bangor for the daily office, and the Stowe Missal, a eucharistic liturgy from an Irish monastery, probably date from around 800. Both these works are in Latin, the liturgical language used in the monasteries of Ireland and Britain, and in most respects they closely follow the Roman rites used in Continental Europe. The Bangor Antiphonary additionally contains a number of prose collects which seem to be direct borrowings from Spain and a collection of Latin hymns which are almost certainly of Irish origin. The Stowe Missal follows the basic framework of the Roman ordinary of the Mass with some Gallican and Spanish features and distinctive Irish elements in the form of penitential prayers and commemorations of local saints. While there were clearly some local variations, there is little reason to suppose that the pattern of worship followed by Celtic Christian communities in the British Isles differed in any significant respect from that found throughout Western Christendom in the early Middle Ages.

Many of the so-called Celtic prayers which have become so popular in recent years, and which have so greatly enriched the worship of many denominations with their colour, rhythm and vivid poetic imagery, do not, in fact, reflect either the liturgical practice or the theology of early Celtic Christianity, in so far as we can discern it. This is particularly true of the material collected by Alexander Carmichael in the

latter half of the nineteenth century that has found its
way into so many modern anthologies of Celtic
prayers. Carmichael's observation in the preface to
the first volume of his *Carmina Gadelica* that 'some of
the hymns may have been composed within the
cloistered cells of Derry and Iona' is, I fear, a case of
romantic fancy getting the better of historical accu-
racy.[1] There were, of course, no cloisters in the
monasteries of Iona or Derry in the time of Columba
and his followers and it is very doubtful if there were
any prayers of the kind found in the *Carmina*. The
notion of a sacred deposit of Celtic Christian prayers
and poems laid down in the sixth and seventh
centuries and still surviving largely unchanged after
nearly one and a half millennia of oral transmission
from generation to generation, however appealing, is
difficult to sustain. Those few prayers and poems
which do survive from early Irish and Scottish
monasteries, such as the material from Iona recently
translated and brought together by Thomas Clancy
and Gilbert Markus in their excellent volume, *Iona –
the Earliest Poetry of a Christian Monastery*, are on the
whole very much starker and darker in tone, more
centred on the themes of sin and judgement and less
affirmative of the natural world than the altogether
gentler verses found in the *Carmina*. Unlike the
tradition of praise poetry which does seem to run
as a continuous thread in Welsh Christian
literature throughout the centuries, there is a marked
discontinuity in both theme and subject matter

between early and later material from Ireland and Scotland.

So what was worship like in the days of Patrick, Columba, David and Aidan? Was it culture-friendly, as many contemporary enthusiasts for Celtic Christianity want to argue, the equivalent of today's 'raves in the naves' and alternative services, or counter-cultural? I have come to the conclusion, after considering the evidence that we have, that it was both. Perhaps the most striking characteristic of Celtic Christian worship was its two-tier nature. In the monasteries it was austere, distant, mysterious, in some ways even rather forbidding, with an ethereal and other-worldly quality. Among the people gathered at the foot of the high standing crosses or in their homes, it was almost certainly much simpler and more earthy, probably involving considerable use of symbol, visual aids and popular vernacular forms of poetry and song.

As with so many other aspects of the life of the early Christian communities in the British Isles, we know much more about the kind of worship that went on within the monastic *vallum* than what happened outside it. We can gain a fairly clear picture from saints' lives and other monastic records of the pattern of worship in communities like Clonmacnoise, Iona, Lindisfarne and Llantwit Major. It centred around the daily and nightly offices which took place at the appointed canonical hours in the simple wooden building that served as the monastic

church. Five times during the day, at the hours
of prime, terce, sext, nones and vespers, and three
times during the hours of darkness, at nightfall, at
midnight and very early in the morning towards
daybreak, the monks gathered, summoned by a bell.
By far the greatest part of each office consisted of
chanting the Psalms in Latin. Irish monks seem to
have worked their way through the entire cycle of
150 psalms more quickly than those in Continental
orders. They sang more of them at each service and
they also met together more often to worship during
the night. Benedictine monks had only two night-
time offices and were able to enjoy eight hours
of unbroken sleep, a luxury denied to their Irish
counterparts. In this respect, as in so many others,
Celtic monastic practice followed that of the Egyptian
desert communities, some of whose members
are described as continually chanting the Psalms.
There are echoes of this practice in the depiction
of Columba in the twelfth-century Irish *Life*
rattling through all 150 psalms (the 'three fifties')
before sunrise every morning as he lay on the beach
on Iona after sleeping for just a few hours on the
bare earth floor of his cell with a stone for his
pillow:

> The three fifties, a heavy burden,
> throughout the night, great was the pain,
> in the sea alongside Scotland,
> before the sun would rise.

Clearly he would lay himself
in the sand – it was a heavy labour,
the outline of his ribs through his garment
was evident when the wind blew.[2]

While the recitation of the psalms, presumably to
some kind of plainsong chant, formed the major part
of the monastic office, there were also Scripture
readings, prayers and hymns. It is in the quality and
quantity of hymns sung that we perhaps find the
most distinctive feature of worship in the early Irish
Church. They seem to have been both more prevalent
and of greater literary merit than the hymns sung in
Continental monasteries. A reference in Adamnan's
Life of Columba to 'a book of the week's hymns'
written out by the saint in his own hand suggests that
the Iona monks had their own weekly cycle of hymns
as well as psalms.[3] It is not clear from this reference
whether Columba was the book's author or merely
its copier but other early tradition suggests that he
was a hymn writer and the earliest source on his life,
the *Amra Choluimb Chille* (Elegy of Colum Cille),
probably written within a few years of his death by
an Irish poet, speaks of him going 'with two songs to
heaven'.[4] Of the many hymns which have been
attributed to Columba, the most likely actually to
have been his own work is the *Altus Prosator*, a deep
theological musing on the mystery of God, the
reality of hell and the Fall. The Antiphonary of Bangor
contains a rich collection of Latin hymns, most of

which are thought to be by sixth- and seventh-century Irish authors. They include a fine eucharistic hymn, *Sancti venite*, two hymns on the life of Christ, *Hymnum dicat* and *Praecamur patrem*, and hymns in honour of Irish saints. While several of the hymns seem derivative of the style of Continental Latin hymn writers like Prudentius, Fortunatus and Ambrose, there are some distinctive touches. A hymn in honour of the martyrs, *Sacratissimi martyres*, is in a metre unknown in early Latin hymnody and seems to owe more to the more accentual and rhythmic verse-forms of early Irish poetry. Its theme of spiritual warfare and the importance of martyrdom also strikes a characteristic Celtic note.

The rhythmic quality of the hymns must have tempered the somewhat austere atmosphere of worship in monastic chapels. There were few visual adornments to distract the monks from their heavily word-centred worship. This is not to say that visual imagery and symbol were absent from the monasteries. The extraordinary delicate and detailed illustrated pages in the great illuminated Gospel books almost certainly served a devotional purpose. Although their precise use and significance is a matter of debate, there is general agreement among scholars that they functioned as icons, being full of theological symbolism and enabling those who gazed on them to enter into deeper meditation and contemplation and let themselves be transported from the earthly to the heavenly realm. There were, of course, long periods of the day when the monks were engaged in their own private devotions, which could involve copying pages of the Psalter and the Gospels.

It is unlikely that the exquisite artwork of the Book of Kells and the other illuminated Gospels and Psalters was seen by those living outside the monasteries. In general, the monks' devotional life seems to have been kept quite separate from the worship of the people. The Eucharist was celebrated privately by the monks at the daily midday service of sext. Even at the major Sunday celebrations of the Mass, there was a sense of two-tier worship. On Iona, for example, the service up to the reading of the Gospel was conducted in the open air outside the chapel where lay members, catechumens, penitents and visitors remained while the monks processed into the church with the presiding priest for the actual communion. This sense of the apartness and otherness of monastic worship must have been reinforced by the fact that it took place entirely in Latin, a language that would have been unintelligible to the great majority of the population. Celtic monastic worship was far from being a model for inclusive, lay-led, participatory, congregation-friendly liturgy. If anything, indeed, it inclined strongly in the opposite direction, being firmly and exclusively clerical, preserving a strong sense of mystery and keeping the people at a distance.

We know much less about what kind of worship took place outside the monastic churches. The monks and clergy who went out into the community baptising, celebrating communion, ministering *viaticum* to the sick and burying the dead probably used fixed liturgies for these various offices and such evidence as we have, like the office for visiting the sick appended to the Book of Deer, suggests that in general they followed Roman rites with some minor local variations. There is some evidence that outdoor services were held, especially perhaps at wells and springs associated with saints. Whether these were led by clergy or lay people, and the extent to which there was a culture of popular devotion using hymns and prayers in the vernacular, it is almost impossible to say. What is clear is that the home became an important place of worship for many people. This may well have been in part a consequence of the lack of parish churches and clergy and later on of the remoteness from such institutions and personnel of many rural communities. It may also have reflected a more positive theme in Celtic worship which found the heavenly in the earthly, the spiritual in the ordinary and everyday, and did not find it necessary to have special buildings in which to worship God. Certainly the *Carmina Gadelica* points to a thriving domestic devotional life and suggests the home was in many ways the main locus of worship, as reflected in the many blessings associated with such tasks as milking the cow and smooring down the fire at night.

There has been much speculation about the

possible role of the high standing crosses as meeting places for worship. Unfortunately we cannot be sure whether people gathered at them for open-air services or whether their role was rather to mark ecclesiastical sites and establish boundaries. The fact that so many crosses have decorated faces which graphically illustrate Bible stories has led to the suggestion that they were used as catechetical or teaching aids, perhaps to instruct newcomers in the faith. Certain scenes recur again and again on the crosses – Noah in the ark, Abraham's sacrifice of Isaac, Daniel in the lion's den and the three children in the fiery furnace – all dramatic stories from the Bible lending themselves to vivid portrayal.

Storytelling was almost certainly an important means of teaching the Christian faith in the British Isles in the early medieval period. The fact that the monks often seem to have gone out on preaching tours armed only with Gospel books suggests that, like Jesus, they relied heavily on parables, supplemented perhaps by the dramatic Old Testament narratives depicted on the high crosses. Illiteracy was widespread and both mission and worship were most probably carried out through the media of story, picture and song. We know that the bardic tradition of expressing the community's myths and legends through song and story was particularly strong in both Anglo-Saxon and Celtic culture. The best-known example of a Christian bard was, of course, Caedmon, who was called in a dream to sing

God's praises and spent the rest of his life in the *monasterium* over which Hilda presided at Whitby, where he fulfilled the role of singer-songwriter in residence, composing songs and poems based on the major themes of the Bible, from the creation story to the Last Judgement.

Early Celtic Christian worship must surely have had a distinctive poetic dimension. The austere psalmody of the monks was alleviated by the introduction of hymns which were noticeably more rhythmic and accented than those of the Continental Latin tradition. The earliest known manuscript of Scottish church music, the Inchcolm Antiphoner, includes chants to celebrate the feast of Columba sung by monks in the twelfth century which musicologists think may go back in some instances to the eighth or even seventh century. They have an altogether freer and more ethereal sound than that of standard Gregorian chant. John Purser, the leading authority on the history of Scottish music, has pointed to the 'Celtic' characteristics of the Inchcolm chants, notably their similarity to traditional Gaelic song and their formal patterning and interweaving which he finds reminiscent of the artwork found in the Book of Kells and on Pictish crosses.[5]

It is significant that nearly all of the earliest extant Celtic prayers are couched in the form of poems rather than prose, with short lines, sometimes rhyming, and regular metres. This is true, for example, of early prayers from Iona like *Adiutor*

laborantium, Noli Pater and Cantemus in omni die, a striking
hymn to Mary written by a monk around 700 which
seems to have been designed for antiphonal singing,
the early Welsh praise poems and Irish prayers like St
Patrick's Breastplate and 'Be thou my vision'. While
some of this material was for formal liturgical use,
most of it surely belonged to a more popular
tradition and was used in private devotion rather
than in formal church services. This is even more true
of the great corpus of material collected towards
the end of the nineteenth century by Alexander
Carmichael in the Scottish Highlands and islands and
by Douglas Hyde in Ireland. Much of it reflects a
tradition of popular devotion focused on the home
and the workplace rather than the church service. The
prayers which fill the Carmina Gadelica and the Religious
Songs of Connacht are for reciting in the kitchen, the
bedroom, the milking parlour and the fishing boat
rather than in the pew. They belong to that culture of
benediction explored in Chapter 2 in which the
ordinary and everyday was hallowed and lifted to
God and in which the forces of evil were seen as
tangible realities which could only be kept at bay by
invoking God's protection. They are often intensely
individualistic and personal.

In this respect, they mirror the individualism of
some of the earliest Celtic prayers. Once again, one
is struck by the twin-track approach to worship
in Celtic Christianity. There is the grand cosmic,
theological sweep of monastic prayer, summed up by

Columba's majestic *Altus Prosator*, and there is the intensely personal vulnerability and humility of another prayer often attributed to the same saint:

> I beg that me, a little man
> Trembling and most wretched,
> Rowing through the infinite storm
> Of this age,
> Christ may draw after Him to the lofty
> Most beautiful haven of life.[6]

Is there anything in the Celtic liturgical tradition which can help us to improve the quality and experience of the worship that we offer to God today?

Perhaps the first thing to note is that in the monasteries at least, and quite possibly elsewhere, Celtic worship was a good deal more austere and very much less up-beat and jolly than many modern church services. There was considerably more awe and reverence and much less chatty informality. If we are to take the monastic model as our guide, following the Celtic way means having more order and awe in our services. It also means recovering that sound that we so seldom hear in contemporary worship, the sound of silence. It is significant how many people say that they prefer visiting churches when they are empty and offer space and quiet for meditation, reflection and prayer rather than when they are full of the ceaseless chatter which precedes most modern services and the endless noise that fills them. There are hopeful signs that many clergy are trying to restore the sound of silence to worship – one is the notice now increasingly to be found pinned on church boards or printed on orders of service which carries the excellent advice: 'Before the service, speak to God. During the service, let God to speak to you. After the service, speak to one another.' Columbanus would have approved of this dictum. In his first sermon he preached that 'God should be looked for in silence, through faith, through righteous living and through prayer'.[7]

In several respects worship in Celtic languages and cultures has continued to preserve the qualities of awesomeness, austerity and reverence which have been largely lost in English and North American churches. In a letter to me following my book on Columba, Andrew Herrick, a clergyman in the Church of Wales, pointed to a significant difference between the hymnody of the English- and Welsh-speaking congregations which make up his bilingual parish. The English hymn tunes are predominantly jolly, in a major key and move on at a hearty pace. The Welsh tunes, by contrast, are often in a minor key, more plaintive and are taken more slowly with a lingering on the last note. For Andrew Herrick, these differences illustrate the deeper and more humble spirituality of the Welsh, who are less confident and comfortable in their worship than their English-speaking neighbours but no less fervent or profound. There are similar qualities in the worship in the Gaelic-speaking congregations of the Church of Scotland, the Free Church and the Free Presbyterian Church in the Western Isles. In my book on Columba, I suggested that the services in these churches, to modern mainland taste so forbidding in their austerity and severe simplicity, probably come as close as any in modern times to the spirit of the worship on Iona in the sixth and seventh centuries.

I think of the atmosphere of the little church on the island of Berneray where I was privileged to spend ten weeks as locum minister some years ago. Instead of the buzz of idle chatter which precedes most church services nowadays, there is an almost palpable stillness as worshippers take their places up to twenty minutes or so before the start of the service and sit in silent prayer and contemplation without any visual or aural distraction, there being neither musical instuments nor decorations of any kind in the church. There is an atmosphere of solemn awe and reverence before the mystery of God. The sung parts of the service consist, as they did in the Irish monasteries, predominantly of the unaccompanied chanting of the Psalms, though in this case in Gaelic or English rather than Latin. Gaelic metrical psalmody, with its pentatonic scale, grace notes, nasal delivery and mournful cadences which seem to rise and fall in time with the rhythm of the sea, bears certain resemblances to the descriptions given of the chanting of psalms by the early monks on Iona. It is also uncannily similar to the style of psalm singing still practised by Coptic monks in Egypt. It may well be, indeed, that preserved in the remote extremities of ancient Christendom, in its eastern desert and western Celtic fringes which we know were once so closely linked, are the remnants of a once universal Christian chant which may well have derived from the synagogue and have been used by our Lord himself in his own worship.

Making greater use of the Psalms is undoubtedly one of the main ways in which we can become more 'Celtic' in our worship today. We do not need to go as far as the 'Wee Frees' and certain other Scottish denominations and banish everything but unaccompanied metrical psalmody from the sanctuary. There are other ways to sing the Psalms and there are other things to sing alongside the Psalms in worship. As we have already noted, Irish monks followed Paul's injunctions and sang hymns and spiritual songs as well as psalms. Psalmody, however, was the bedrock of their daily devotions. So it was, indeed, for virtually all the churches of the British Isles until the nineteenth century when hymns came to supplant the monopoly of metrical psalmody. There is no doubt that singing hymns and worship songs has enormously enhanced the liveliness of modern worship. It has unfortunately also often meant a squeezing out of the Psalms and, more seriously, a narrowing of the range of emotions expressed in worship. Most hymns and worship songs, like most of the few psalms that are still regularly sung in services, are predominantly upbeat, focused on praise and calculated to promote the feel-good factor. Few of them express the feelings of dejection, doubt, lament, anger and confusion which underlie a good many of the Psalms. These feelings need to be expressed and articulated in worship.

A movement is afoot in a number of different denominations to make much more use of the Psalms in worship, and especially those which express negative and difficult emotions and are not simply upbeat songs of praise and adoration. One of the most important initiatives in this area has come from the Iona Community's Wild Goose Worship Group, led by John Bell, whose collection, *Psalms of Patience, Protest and Praise*, provides modern translations and musical settings of psalms expressing a wide range of emotions. In a very different musical idiom, Ian White has produced contemporary versions of nearly all the Psalms for performance. The Free Church of Scotland has recently issued a new metrical Psalter and the Church of Scotland is committed to providing versions of the Psalms in a variety of different styles for congregational use as part of its new hymnal.

Another feature of monastic liturgy which is undergoing a significant revival today is the daily office. Christians of many different traditions are rediscovering the spiritual benefits of saying a daily office both in the context of public worship and as a private devotional exercise. *Celebrating Common Prayer*, based on the Franciscan office, is now in widespread use throughout the Church of England. The Church of Scotland's latest (1994) *Book of Common Order* for the first time contains a daily office for both morning and evening use 'to encourage the discipline of daily private devotion'.[8] The office, which is offered for use either by individuals on their own or by families and small groups, was especially requested by those training for the ministry. A growing number of churches are introducing short daily weekday services, often around lunchtime, and there also seems to be a significant increase in the number of people saying their own daily offices at home. Recent years have seen a proliferation of books providing daily prayers and readings, often with a Celtic flavour. They include the *Celtic Daily Office* and *Celtic Night Office* from the Northumbria Community, Ray Simpson's *Celtic Daily Prayers*, Philip Newell's weekly cycle of prayers from Iona Abbey, *Each Day and Each Night*, and David Adam's *Rhythms of Life*. How far the largely modern and entirely English-language material gathered in these collections is in any real sense Celtic is a moot point. It is a major manifestation of the current wave of Celtic Christian revivalism, which like earlier such movements involves creative reconstruction and invention, and Celtic scholars may legitimately question its authenticity and faithfulness to Gaelic and Welsh traditions. What there can be no gainsaying, however, is that it restores that rhythm of prayer that was so central and strking a feature of Celtic Christianity.

We are, indeed, witnessing the recovery of the Celtic rhythm of prayer in two senses. As well as an increase in the discipline of regular daily devotion reminiscent of (though much less taxing than) the daily rhythm of prayer at the heart of the *monasterium*, there is also a welcome move in many churches to have a more rhythmic, poetic style of prayer in public worship. Several enthusiasts for Celtic Christianity, myself included, have contrasted the poetic quality of its prayer with the much more long-winded and prosy character of Anglo-Saxon prayer. The late Martin Reith summed up the difference by talking about the tuppence-coloured poetry of the Celts and the penny-plain prose of the Anglo-Saxons. I am increasingly persuaded that this is an unfair and over-simplistic distinction. There are some beautiful and highly poetic prayers in the Anglo-Saxon and later English traditions and some of the most cumbersome and prose-laden prayers that I have ever heard have been delivered extempore by ministers in the churches of the Western Isles whose style of worship I have just compared to that of Columba's Iona. There is no doubt, however, that Celtic Christianity has given us some particularly striking examples of short, rhythmic prayers which speak with both a directness and a rich use of imagery and illustration in a way that is often not found in the longer, more complex and conceptual prayers of the Germanic and Latin traditions which have influenced so much of our worship. This imaginative poetic trait can be seen in early Irish prayers like St Patrick's Breastplate as well as in much later material like the Gaelic blessings in the *Carmina Gadelica*. It is this authentically (though not exclusively) Celtic note which is sounded by the modern prayers of Ray Simpson and David Adam with their rhythmic form, vivid imagery and short, often repeated phrases.

It is striking how many of these rhythmic prayers, both of wholly modern construction and also re-workings and translations of older material originally in Irish or Scots Gaelic, Welsh or Latin, are finding their way into the services of many churches. The Church of Scotland's new *Book of Common Order* contains both an order for morning service and for the celebration of communion which incorporate elements from older Celtic material and new prayers written in a consciously 'Celtic' style. It is not uncommon for lightly adapted material from the *Carmina Gadelica* to feature in wedding, baptism and funeral services as well as in regular Sunday worship and Irish benedictions (notably the one which begins 'May the road rise to meet you') are increasingly popular at the end of services. These simple prayers with their rhythmic cadences and vivid physical imagery do seem to speak to both churched and unchurched people in a way that other modern liturgical language does not. They are often relatively easy to memorise and lend themselves to being used responsively. Leading contemporary liturgists like Michael Perham are calling for the recovery of the art of writing rhythmically and poetically.[9] The pastoral value of these prayers has already been noted. They also have considerable liturgical value.

If poetry is coming back into our worship, then so also is story and song. A whole new school of hermeneutics is now proclaiming that the way to reach a modern congregation is by telling stories. Metanarrative may be one of the casualties of post-modernism but mini-narratives, in the sense of vivid, dramatic stories told in the tradition of Jesus' parables and children's yarns, are very much in favour. The Celts, like other peoples having a predominantly oral culture, were, of course, great storytellers and this tradition spread over into their Christian worship and evangelism. There is much interest now, not least in the flourishing alternative worship scene, in the idea of worship as ceilidh, focused around telling stories and singing songs which celebrate the identity and values of those taking part as well as articulating their faith and carrying their praise and petitions to God. Ray Simpson describes Hilda's monastery at Whitby hosting the first recorded Christian karaokes as Caedmon led the community in singalongs. This dimension of Celtic worship, found outside the confines of the sanctuary but within the wider sacred space of the *monasterium*, needs to be acknowledged and affirmed alongside the more austere and awe-filled atmosphere of the monastic offices.

We have already noted that one of the distinguishing features of worship in the Irish monasteries and their offshoots in Scotland, Wales and northern England was the quality and quantity of the hymns sung. It is reasonable to assume that song played a major part in the more informal and domestic devotions of people worshipping God in their homes, their workplaces or gathered together at the foot of the high standing crosses or at the site of a sacred well or spring. Song in many different varieties has been one of the most significant and ubiquitous new features in worship over recent years. It has come in all sorts of forms – charismatic choruses, contemporary worship songs, chants from Taizé and Iona and songs from the worldwide Church, notably both in translation and in their original languages from Africa, Latin America and Asia. Some of us are deeply uneasy at the ousting of hymns in some churches to make way for an exclusive diet of songs – and there is no reason why the former should disappear and be supplanted by the latter – but there is no doubt that the introduction of songs into worship has enhanced the experience of worship for many people.

As with prayers, there has been a huge proliferation of 'Celtic' Christian music in recent years. Much of it uses the pre-Christian sound of the drums and harps which would have ushered in the feasts of Beltane and Samhaine. Indeed, Celtic Christian bands like Iona, Why?, the Electrics and Skelling, and soloists like Sammy Horner and David Fitzgerald have an explicit agenda of redeeming pagan music and baptising it for Christ. In this they are following the example of the Celtic saints who baptised pagan shrines and wells. How far their various blends of folk, rock, soul, dance music and easy listening even remotely approximate to the music that accompanied Celtic worship in the seventh or eighth centuries, or even the seventeenth and eighteenth, it is, perhaps, better not to ask. Their purpose is not so much to re-create the sound and style of authentic Celtic worship but rather to proclaim the gospel and praise the Lord in a way that is culturally friendly today and taps into the current enthusiasm for Celtic music, whatever that might be.

This kind of contemporary Christian music may play an important role in reconnecting us with ancient means of altering consciousness and attaining a state of ecstasy. In common with the rituals of other so-called primitive cultures, pre-Christian Celtic worship made much use of drumming, chanting and dancing to enable people to step out of their everyday worlds into the spiritual realm. How far these techniques were taken up by the churches is very doubtful. They were probably condemned as they have been throughout most of Western

Christendom. With these traditional routes to altered
consciousness and spiritual ecstasy closed off, people
have increasingly turned to much more damaging
alternatives like drugs and alcohol. In restoring drum
beats and dance rhythms, contemporary Celtic
Christian bands are reminding us of a dimension of
worship that we have all but lost – the altering of
consciousness which allows those who are earthbound to be transported towards heaven. I have long
felt that a more numinous style of worship filled with
awe and mystery might reduce the demand for
artificial stimulants and mind-altering drugs. This is
not the place to ride that particular hobby horse, but
it is worth noting the contribution that Celtic
Christian bands may be making in this area.

Of rather more dubious 'Celticity' are those
best-selling CDs with titles like 'Celtic expressions of
worship' which give pan pipes and harp accompani-
ments to quintessentially English Victorian hymns
like 'The day thou gavest, Lord, is ended' and 'The
King of love my shepherd is'. I suppose that as an
unashamed and unabashed enthusiast for Victorian
hymns I ought to be grateful for anything that
promotes them and gives them a new audience and
lease of life. Among the latest manifestations of what
one might call the Celtic make-over syndrome are a
set of CDs with the titles *Celtic Tranquillity*, *Celtic
Reflections* and *Celtic Moods*. If, as I suspect that their
producers and promoters would claim, they come
into the category of easy listening and music for

relaxation, then perhaps they too should be welcomed as providing a substitute to tranquillisers and anti-depressant drugs.

Rather closer, perhaps, to the spirit of Celtic devotion, at least in some of its more popular expressions, are the modern songs written by members of the Iona Community like John Bell, Graham Maule and Kathy Galloway. Several of these pick up themes and phrases from ancient Irish prayers ('Today I arise and Christ is beside me') or use traditional folk tunes, like 'Dream Angus' for 'A touching place' or 'Pulling Bracken' for 'Dance and sing all creation'. Most authentic of all the new Celtic worship songs are those which directly translate ancient texts and retain their original tunes, like James Quinn's 'The seed is Christ's' from *An Chreost an sheil*. It is perhaps significant, and certainly encouraging, that one song which falls firmly into this last category, Eleanor Hull's 'Be thou my vision', regularly appears near the top in polls of favourite hymns.

As well as welcoming more poetry, story and song into worship, we are also beginning to introduce more symbolism. Symbols are very important in contemporary popular culture and spirituality, as witnessed by the way grieving is so often expressed through leaving objects at what effectively become shrines – football scarves and strips at the site of the Hillsborough disaster, flowers, teddy bears and bottles of champagne outside the gates of Kensington

Palace after the death of Diana, Princess of Wales. Churches are often understandably ambivalent about this kind of activity, which seems to border on idolatry. Yet perhaps we should be incorporating these and other symbols of popular devotion and affection into our rituals and worship much as the Celtic saints blessed pagan wells and turned them into Christian shrines. Churches have long consecrated and hallowed national and tribal emblems in the form of flags and banners, and the lighting of candles remains one of the most meaningful ways in which people can symbolically express their prayers.

Increasingly, dance, drama, artwork, sculpture and multimedia presentations are being used in worship. As we have seen, the Celtic high standing crosses with their elaborately carved and possibly coloured depictions of biblical episodes almost certainly served as visual aids and pointers to worship and the illuminated manuscripts had an iconic function. There is growing interest within Western Christianity in the theology and spirituality of icons, and several churches use them both in public services of worship and as aids for personal devotion. Imaginatively conceived and used, the video clip or computer-generated graphic perhaps provides the modern equivalent of the illuminated manuscript or painted icon as a visual symbol which can become a medium for meditation and spiritual transformation.

It is in the developing area of experimental and alternative worship that visual media and symbols are being used most extensively and creatively. Services often taking place late in the evening and aimed predominantly at those in their late teens and twenties mix dance music, laser shows and video projection alongside more traditional forms of prayer and meditation. Celtic Christianity has been a major influence on several alternative services, notably in the area of prayer where much use is made of *Carmina Gadelica*-style material, but also more generally in the culture-friendly approach which incorporates popular contemporary symbols and forms. The Glasgow Late Late service, one of the longest running and most rooted in the alternative worship scene, uses the Celtic liturgies of the Iona Community together with video-projected images and more traditional symbols like candles and stained glass. There is a strong physical dimension to the worship with dance and mime and the laying on of hands for healing. Much use is also made of natural objects like dried flowers, pine cones, stones, water and earth. While contemporary music in various styles features prominently in the Late Late Service, so also does the sound of silence.

Creative imagination informs much of what is happening, not just in the alternative worship scene but in the refreshment and reinvigoration of traditional worship. There is also sadly a good deal of pure gimmickry, cosy, chatty informality and dumbed-down mateyness. It is very tempting in the age of the soundbite, the soap opera and the tabloid to make worship a branch of the light entertainment industry and turn services into a series of humorous sketches and 'turns' compèred by the clerical equivalent of a chat-show host. This may be the way for some people to encounter God, but it does not engage their deeper emotions and spiritual yearnings even in our post-modern, pick-and-mix religious supermarket. It is most emphatically not the Celtic way of worship. Whatever we take as most characteristic – the austerity of monastic plainchant, the majestic severity of Columba's *Altus Prosator*, the exquisite mystical symbolism of the Book of Kells, the deep cry for God's protection in the breastplate prayers and hymns, or the gentle, intimate, affirmative blessings in the *Carmina Gadelica* – there is nothing remotely contrived or meretricious in Celtic worship. It is heartfelt, honest, serious and utterly focused on the trinitarian Godhead.

How can we avoid dumbing down worship while making it fresh and meaningful today? Perhaps one way is to return to the model of the *monasterium* as the 'colony of heaven' in which a disciplined ritual of prayer and formal liturgy can undergird and nourish those involved in more experimental forms of worship in the community. The *monasterium*, whether cathedral, parish church or other institution, provides the still and stable centre, the pool of prayer, psalmody and spirituality from which all can drink and refresh themselves. It sets standards, provides a model of liturgical excellence and preserves awe and reverence at the heart of worship. Some will want no more than this. Others, at different stages of their faith journey, will feel the need to express themselves to God in other less formal and traditional ways. In congregations, cells and house groups connected to the *monasterium* like spokes of a wheel to the hub, they will be able to engage in more innovative and experimental worship.

To some extent this model already operates in various ways. The best alternative worship services, like the Glasgow Late Late service, are linked to established churches which also maintain more traditional patterns of worship. In the Iona Community, services in the Abbey are both splendid and awesome, although anything but static and hidebound. Members and associates, meeting in family groups in one another's homes and other more intimate settings, are linked to the Abbey liturgy through the recitation of the Iona office but are also free to devise their own ways of worship. Jennyfields Church in Harrogate, a relatively recent church-plant in a new housing area, holds its worship service early on a Saturday evening in a junior school. This time was found to suit the young and largely unchurched congregation, many of whom come to the service on their way to a night out. More formal and traditional Sunday morning worship is provided in Jennyfields' mother church, St Wilfrid's, a Grade 1 listed building in the centre of the spa town. This pattern of formal services provided in the monasterium with more experimental and informal worship taking place in church plants, cells and other small groups is surely the way forward in many places.

Perhaps the crucial lesson that we have to learn from Celtic Christianity is the importance of balance and rhythm in worship as in so much else. There needs to be room for both awe and intimacy, silence and celebration, relevance and transcendence, order and spontaneity. But how can we hold these apparent opposites together and not lean so far towards one that we lose the other? I suspect that the answer may lie in adopting the twin-track approach that I am more and more convinced characterised the Celtic Christian model of worship. This might take some of the sting out of the rather unedifying and sometimes ill-tempered debates between traditionalists and modernisers, élitists and populists, proponents of timeless transcendence and apostles of relevance. The austerity, awe and formality of monastic liturgy existed alongside popular devotions in homes and at outdoor gatherings which may well have had pagan elements and certainly had an earthy simplicity and intimacy. There was no attempt to merge the two and create blanket all-age, inclusive services which mixed the formal and the informal, the timeless and the contemporary, the clerical and the popular. We should likewise not be trying either to merge or to set against each other traditional church services and contemporary, praise-filled worship. There is no call

to snipe at cathedral choral evensong for being élitist
and inaccessible to many. So was the worship in
Celtic monasteries. Nor is there any call to condemn
modern worship songs and choruses as simplistic
repetitive ditties. So were many of the prayers and
charms used by Hebridean crofters and fishing folk
in their homes and places of work. Both styles of
worship are equally honest and valid expressions of
the deep-seated human instinct to communicate with
God and voice petitions and praise. They reflect the
fact that people are on different stages of their faith
journeys and express their worship in radically
different ways.

The Celtic twin-track model can perhaps also help
us to resolve the question as to whether worship
should be culture-friendly or counter-cultural. Celtic
Christian worship had two main *loci* – the monastery
and the home. The liturgy in the monastery was
anything but culture-friendly, even if the monasteries
were. It was in Latin, a language inaccessible and
unintelligible to most, involved lengthy chanting
of the Psalms and had no elements of lay participation or spontaneity. The prayers which people said
in their own homes, by contrast, were in the
vernacular and centred around everyday tasks like
milking the cow, lighting the fire or preparing for
bed. These two modes of worshipping God existed
side by side. They were not fused to create a lowest
common denominator service trying to be all things
to all people and ending up meaning nothing to

Colonies of Heaven

anyone. This is a message that we need to heed. The drive to all-age worship incorporating bits of this and that, traditional and modern, produces pot-pourris that are often exclusive rather than inclusive.

Much worship is now once again going on in homes and among small cell groups, especially in the new church movement. But what of corporate public worship in church? Too often it is dreary, predictable and dull. We need a new paradigm of public worship. The traditional pattern which moves through adoration, confession, thanksgiving and supplication is stale and tired. The adoration is too often formulaic and uninspiring, the confession, as we have already noted, is often too vague and unfocused to be very meaningful, the thanksgiving can sound like a thankyou letter and the supplication or intercession like a Cook's tour round the world's disaster areas. Robert Warren has suggested a new paradigm for worship with a threefold dynamic of celebration, lament and hope.[10] This has a strongly Celtic resonance. Celebration gives liturgical form to the Celtic emphasis on benediction, proclaiming the primary goodness of the world in the spirit of the Welsh tradition of praise poetry. Lament as both an individual and communal activity is, of course, a fundamental motif in the Psalms, which were so central to Celtic monastic worship, and also reflects its profoundly penitential strain. Hope is perhaps the theme that we most need to recover in contemporary

[154]

worship. All too often it is the missing ingredient in our services. Just as confession of a rather vague and inappropriate kind is so often left hanging without a proper assurance of absolution and forgiveness, so long litanies of woes are often recited without any proclamation of the great Christian value of hope. This aspect of contemporary worship has been well identified and described by the writer and broadcaster, Angela Tilby:

> I have been struck by the overwhelmingly depressing note of the intercessions offered in many churches. Is it too much of a distortion to suggest that typically we bemoan the tragic divisions of the Church; the conflicts and sufferings of the world; instances of misery and grief in the local community; sickness and death in the parish; and anxiety and doubt in the mind of the congregation? No thanksgiving, no hope, no note of expectation or confidence in deliverance.
>
> Christ is available only as a vulnerable, tragic figure, present only in pain. This Christ empathises with us, but cannot do anything to save us because he is totally earthbound and timebound. He fixes our eyes on sadness, so that we end up admiring our own misery as a kind of virtue.[11]

I freely confess to being one of those many modern theologians who has dwelt much on the suffering Christ (and particularly in my case on the sacrificing God). I think it is probably true to say that those of us who take services in traditional mainstream churches are sometimes easier with suffering, pain and angst than with joy and hope. This partly springs from a deep unease with the rather shallow feel-good factor of some contemporary worship material and a sense that it does not really address the ambiguities of the human condition. Worship, like all human activities, is conducted in the shadow of the cross upreared on Calvary with all its darkness and shame. But it is also offered through and to the Christ triumphant, the one who is risen, ascended and glorified, priest and king as well as victim and servant. Those of us who are naturally of a theologically liberal hue perhaps find it particularly hard to embrace and affirm this dimension of the gospel in our worship. We are happier with Jesus the vulnerable marginal Galilean than with Christ the King. We are terrified of triumphalism. We have banished a whole host of hope-filled hymns of encouragement on the grounds that they are shallowly triumphalist. Our determination to be grittily incarnational has made us too earthbound. We preach Jesus the social prophet and man of sorrows. We preach Christ crucified. But we are much less enthusiastic about preaching Christ risen, ascended and glorified. We need, in a phrase which I hear applied to Afro-Caribbean worship in Britain, 'to pray heaven down to earth'.

Celtic worship was not triumphalistic but it had a great sense of the triumph of Christ. The figure of *Christus Victor*, the risen and ascended Jesus, dominates many high standing crosses. The kingship of Christ was a favourite motif in Irish prayers and hymns, hardly surprisingly when kingship was so important a feature of secular life and society. 'Be thou my vision' is typical in its reference to 'the high king of heaven'. Many of the poems that have come down to us from the 'golden age' of Celtic Christianity have a strong eschatological dimension. They look forward to the Second Coming, to the breaking in of heaven on earth, with a sense of anticipation and expectation. Columba's *Altus Prosator*, addressed to the 'High Creator' who looks down 'from the summit of the Kingdom of Heaven, where angels stand', confidently looks forward to the time:

> When Christ, the most high Lord, comes down
> from the heavens,
> The brightest sign and standard of the Cross
> will shine forth.
> The two principal lights being obscured,
> The stars will fall to earth like the fruit of a fig
> tree
> And the face of the world will be like the fire
> of a furnace.
> Then armies will hide in the caves of the
> mountains.

By the singing of hymns eagerly ringing out,
By thousands of angels rejoicing in holy
   dances,
And by the four living creatures full of eyes,
With the twenty-four joyful elders
Casting their crowns under the feet of the
   Lamb of God,
The Trinity is praised in eternal threefold
   exchanges.

The raging anger of fire will devour the
   adversaries
Who will not believe that Christ came from
   God the Father.
But we shall surely fly off to meet him straight
   away,
And thus we shall be with him in several ranks
   of dignities
According to the eternal merits of our rewards,
To abide in glory from age to age.[12]

Apocalyptic, awesome and frightening as all of this
may be to modern eyes, it is also fundamentally filled
with hope. Hope is the ingredient missing from so
much of life today as well as from worship. We need
to celebrate with the Celts the *Christus Victor*, to sing
the great songs of expectation as we march through
the pilgrim land, to point to the glories that are to
come not just in the next world but in this world too
as the Kingdom comes. We need with Columba to

[158]

share in the hymns eagerly ringing out and to join the thousands of angels rejoicing in holy dances. We need above all to have more sense of heaven in our worship and to make the places where we worship, whether churches or homes, colonies of heaven in which earth and heaven meet, the glory shines through the grey, ordinary things are rendered extraordinary and hope keeps breaking through. Then perhaps people will come to worship with a sense of excitement and expectancy rather than out of a sense of duty.

5

The Communion of Saints

Saints are central to Celtic Christianity. Accounts of their lives, written by devoted hagiographers and full of fanciful stories and legends, form one of our most important sources for the history of Christianity in the British Isles between the fifth and seventh centuries. This period, the 'golden age' of Celtic Christianity, is, indeed, often known as the age of saints. It is dominated by the lives and achievements of Patrick, Brigit, Ninian, Columba, Columbanus, David, Aidan and a host of other saintly figures hailed for their superhuman spirituality and sanctity and remembered as the founders of numerous monasteries. Ireland in particular seems to have bred saints in remarkable numbers in this period, coming to be known as the *insula sanctorum*. Indeed, it has been calculated that more saints apparently lived on that small island in two centuries than in the rest of the world in the entire period since.

There are several striking aspects to the Celtic fondness for saints. At one level it betokened a recognition that there are figures of outstanding personal holiness and charisma who stand out as having a particular authority. We are brought back to the inegalitarian streak in Celtic Christianity. Some people were seen as holier than others. It is also striking how many of the Celtic saints seem to have been of aristocratic stock. This is pre-eminently true of Columba, a high-born member of the ruling sept of the powerful O'Neill clan who by all accounts might well have become high king of Ireland had he not taken monastic vows. Many other saints are described by their biographers as being of noble birth – indeed allusion to this aspect of their subjects' lives is so common among Celtic hagiographers as to take on a formulaic quality.

The strong links made between sainthood and noble birth and breeding reflect the values of a society where authority was personal rather than institutional and where leadership was based on ties of loyalty and kinship. In many ways the figure of the noble saint paralleled and complemented that of the godly king. As we have seen, the principle of heredity was very important in Celtic society, and monasteries, almost as much as their secular counterparts the *tuaths* or kingships, were organised into families and run on tribal lines.

It would be wrong, however, to conclude that certain individuals were hailed as saints simply because they came of aristocratic stock and belonged to a natural ruling caste. Qualities of humility, piety and discipleship were more important in the making of Celtic saints. What perhaps comes over above all from their lives is the natural authority that they commanded because of their manifest integrity and charisma. Disciples and followers are portrayed as being attracted to them because, like Christ, they spoke as those having authority. We get a vivid sense of this aspect of sainthood in the stories of the huge crowds which flock to hear David preaching at Ystrad David, necessitating the miraculous rising up of a hill beneath his feet so that he is able to be seen and heard by all. The impression given here, as in so many stories from the lives of the Celtic saints, is of a charisma of holiness and a spiritual authority recognised by the people and not just derived from office or appointment. Not every one of the Celtic saints was in a leadership role, although many were, but all shared an aura of spiritual authority which led them to be respected and looked up to.

Although it was undoubtedly founded on genuine popular devotion and on real lives of outstanding holiness, the creation of the great pantheon of Celtic saints from the fifth and sixth centuries was a wholly retrospective exercise carried out long after their deaths by successive hagiographers who wove ever more fanciful tales of miraculous wonder-working. I have traced the two main eras in this process of saint-making, from the late seventh to the late eighth century and from the late eleventh to the early thirteenth century, in the first two chapters of my book *Celtic Christianity: Making Myths and Dreaming Dreams*. It makes for rather unedifying reading. Individual saints were promoted, their lives written, their miracles made ever more stupendous and their bones encased in order to enhance the claim of a particular monastery, church, cathedral or diocese to pre-eminence over others by giving it a long pedigree and impressive foundation legend, and to promote the interests of a flourishing and lucrative pilgrim trade. As their cults developed, saints were venerated less and less for their personal holiness in life and more and more for their posthumous power to work miracles, bring victory in battle and protect and defend those who adopted them as patrons.

The successive waves of hagiography under which the Celtic saints were submerged by medieval spin-doctors in the cause of ecclesiastical power politics have had a severely distorting effect. They present a picture of spiritual Power Rangers charging around performing spectacular miracles and founding hundreds of churches which is wholly at odds with the evidence that we have from more contemporary sources. We can see the extent of this distortion particularly clearly in the case of Patrick, the only Celtic saint who has actually left us autobiograhical material. His Confessio is, as we have already noted, a testament of utter humility and vulnerability. It is candid about the difficulties he faces in spreading the faith in Ireland and the compromises and deals he has to make with rulers to ensure safe passage for himself and other missionaries through the areas they control. How different is Patrick the saint as he emerges from the lives of him which began to be written two hundred or so years after his death. The almost painfully honest and self-critical author of the Confessio is transformed into the superhuman wonder-worker, performing spectacular miracles wherever he goes, converting everybody in sight and setting up churches left right and centre across the whole of Ireland. Columba underwent a similarly radical image make-over in the centuries following his death. The ascetic monk of Iona becomes the apostle of Scotland, the man who almost single-handedly converted the Picts. The pastor and counsellor becomes the magic man, capable of making a wild boar drop dead in its tracks and turning back the Loch Ness monster as though it was controlled by strings. The 'dove of the church' becomes the talisman of military success, his relics, encased in jewel-encrusted caskets, being paraded in front of Scottish and Irish armies on the eve of battle to ensure their victory.

It is important to note that there was nothing uniquely Celtic in this fascination with saints. As the editors of a recent volume of essays on Columba observe, 'the cult of the saints is one of the defining attributes of the Middle Ages'.[1] Peter Brown has charted how saints' cults developed throughout Latin Christendom, beginning with the veneration of martyrs in the fourth and fifth centuries and spreading so that by the end of the sixth century 'the graves of the saints . . . had become centres of the ecclesiastical life of their region'.[2] Across Europe, growing concern about sin and judgement, possibly stimulated by the rise of the ascetic movement, brought a new emphasis on the need for patrons and friends within the company of heaven. Saints filled this role. With miracle stories demonstrating that their powers extended beyond death, they came to be seen as invisible companions, role models and intimate protectors. The British and Irish hagiographers, many of them of Anglo-Norman background, who built up the protective properties of Patrick, Ninian, Columba, David, Aidan and Cuthbert, were part of a Europe-wide phenomenon.

The medieval mindset that produced the cult of saints is so different from ours that it takes a quantum leap of imagination to begin to understand it. The *Vitae Sanctorum* which celebrated and idolised such figures as Brigit, Patrick, Columba and Aidan in ways that we find so difficult to take seriously exemplify an approach to the lives and character of the famous which is the exact opposite of that adopted by both popular journalists and serious biographers in our own age. In a culture such as ours where no opportunity is missed to denigrate and bring down the reputations of the dead as well as the living, and the search is relentless to expose feet of clay and find skeletons in every cupboard, it is hard to comprehend an attitude of hero-worship and devotion which sought to build up reputations rather than destroy them. Some of the motives which underlay the production of the saints' lives may have been self-seeking, but they were written to point a moral, provide an example and give encouragement to the faithful as well as to support the claims of a particular church or promote a lucrative pilgrim trade. They also reflected a widespread popular mood of devotion in which long-dead saints were as real a presence in people's lives as characters from television soap operas are today. More real, in fact, because the saints could actually do things and help people. As one of the leading modern authorities on medieval saints' cults has written:

> The saints were not fictions created by
> monastic hagiographers to serve a useful end,
> but lively presences who owned property,
> appeared in visions, cured the sick, and
> dispensed justice. Hagiography provided the
> prism through which relics were viewed and
> interpreted, but a literary genre could not
> invent the presence of saintly patrons.[3]

Perhaps the crucial difference between the medieval and the modern mind in this respect lies in their attitudes towards death and the dead. The saints' cults which flourished in the Middle Ages sprang from a belief that the dead live on as a presence in heaven, close to God and surrounding his throne, able to intercede before him on behalf of the living and indeed able to influence events in this world. For medieval Christians the saints were just as real and close a presence in death as they had been in life, indeed in many ways even more so. Only the thinnest of veils separated this world from the next and there was a deep and almost tangible communion between the dead and those still living.

Celtic Christians perhaps had an especially acute sense of the thinness of this veil, thanks to the prominence given in both Irish and Welsh mythology to the 'otherworld' as a realm contained within the known landscape and accessible to human beings. In pre-Christian Celtic tales the otherworld was given various locations: islands in the western ocean (as in the late seventh- or early eighth-century epic *The Voyage of Braan*), under the sea, or under the earth. While the dominant image was of a happy place where the dead live again in a world full of magic, enchantment and music (as in the Irish myth of *Tir na n'Og*, the Land of Forever Young), there was also a darker side of the otherworld, as a sombre place full of death, especially for those who crossed over to it while still alive. This sense of the closeness of the two worlds produced a strong belief in supernatural apparitions both good (fairies, kelpies, sprites) and bad (demons and infernal forces). Many of these beliefs were not lost with the coming of Christianity. The epic story of the navigation of St Brendan Christianises the *Voyage of Braan* and links the pilgrimage to heaven with the old tradition that the otherworld was to be found in the islands of the western ocean. A major pilgrimage centre developed in the late twelfth century on the island on Lough Derg in Donegal where, through the agency of Patrick, visitors were supposedly granted a glimpse into the next world by descending into a cave known as Patrick's Purgatory. Visions of angels, devils and other supernatural apparitions recur again and again in the lives of the Celtic saints.

It was not, of course, just lingering pagan superstitions which made Celtic Christians so aware of angelic presences and intimations of the next world. Early Christians lived in constant contact with supernatural beings, as did the writers of the books that make up the Old and New Testaments. When Adamnan wrote of Columba seeing 'a line of foul black devils armed with iron spikes and drawn up ready for battle' or 'holy angels fighting in the air against the power of the Adversary' he was echoing the language of the Book of Revelation.[4] In seeing the souls of the righteous physically being carried by angels to heaven, Columba himself was sharing the same vision that had animated St Luke's account of the death of Lazarus in the parable of Dives and Lazarus. Celtic Christians read the New Testament a good deal more literally than we do. The great emphasis placed on hospitality in the monasteries derived at least in part from obedience to the injunction in Hebrews 13:2: 'Do not neglect to show hospitality to strangers, for thereby some have entertained angels unawares' (RSV).

Another well-known text from the Epistle to the Hebrews was fundamental to the strong and living doctrine of the Communion of Saints that informed Celtic Christianity: 'Since we are surrounded by so great a cloud of witnesses, let us also lay aside every weight, and sin which clings so closely, and let us run with perseverance the race that is set before us, looking to Jesus the pioneer and perfecter of our faith' (Hebrews 12:1 RSV). Several phrases in this text resonated with distinctive features of Celtic Christianity. The notion of the 'cloud of witnesses' had particular appeal in a monastic culture where martyrdom, understood as costly witness, was so important and where those who had gone before in the faith, having fought the good fight and remained true and faithful to the end, were indeed seen as surrounding those still struggling to persevere on earth. The idea of the cloud of witnesses surrounding and helping those who still had to run with patience the race set before them chimed in with the frequent practice of having an angel or a dead saint as well as a living companion as one's soul friend and fellow-pilgrim.

The verse's overall sense of the compassing and surrounding power of the hosts of heaven, and their closeness to Jesus, is echoed in much Gaelic devotional verse, particularly that found in the *Carmina Gadelica*.

The dead, conceived of both as proper subjects for intercessory prayer and in their role as constituting the Communion of Saints and Church Triumphant, were very much a presence in Celtic Christian worship. One of the obligations recognised by Irish law as being owed by the monasteries to the people was singing psalms and other prayers on behalf of the dead. It was known as 'singing on what is not seen'. Following Augustine, the Irish church divided the dead into those who were so good that they did not need prayers of the living, those who were so wicked that no prayers could help them, and those in between whose lot after death could be affected not just by the prayers of the living but also by their fasts and vigils.[5] Worship was seen as a joint enterprise of the Church Militant and the Church Triumphant, with the Eucharist especially uniting heavenly and earthly worshippers. A fascinating analysis of the Temptation page in the Book of Kells by Heather Pulliam at the Eleventh International Celtic Congress in 1999 showed how Satan is confronted by Christ holding a chalice, with the Church Triumphant at his feet and the Church Militant at his side.

Within Celtic Christianity, the notion of the Communion of Saints had a special rootedness in place and locality. This comes over in the importance of local sites associated with particular saints, in terms of both natural features, like wells and springs, and buildings, such as churches and monasteries. During the Middle Ages, there were far more cults of purely local saints in the British Isles, and especially in Ireland, than in Continental Europe. Local saints' cults developed earlier in these western Celtic extremities of Christendom. There were already a good many in Ireland by the end of the eighth century, whereas on the Continent they were not much in evidence before the ninth century. There is no Continental parallel to the Martyrology of Tallaght, which dates from around 800 and commemorates a very large number of native saints. It is almost certainly because of the proliferation of these local cults that Ireland has such an exceptionally large number of saints. As Professor Padraig O Riain has demonstrated, a relatively small number of actual early saints was almost certainly expanded into a multitude because of the tendency of Irish cults to fragment and localise. Many of those whom we think of as different saints are probably simply variations on the name of a single original.[6] When in the eleventh and twelfth centuries the rest of Europe gradually assumed universal catholic saints, Ireland and Britain continued to venerate local saints, the great majority of whom came from the 'golden age' of Celtic Christianity.

This emphasis on saints as protectors and patrons

of particular localities has continued to be a marked feature of the Christian life of the Celtic regions of the British Isles to this day. So also has a sense of their close continuing presence and a wider appreciation of the protective powers of both saints and angels. Alongside prayers of the *lorica* or breastplate and the *caim* or encircling variety, there has been a long tradition of Gaelic invocations of the saints, angels and archangels as protectors against both physical and spiritual dangers. A still popular Irish prayer said by those settling down to sleep for the night invokes the four angels guarding the corners of the bed. In similar vein is this verse from 'I lie in my bed' in the *Carmina Gadelica*:

> Uriel shall be at my feet
> Ariel shall be at my back,
> Gabriel shall be at my head,
> And Raphael shall be at my side.[7]

Many of the prayers in the *Carmina* call on the joint help of archangels, local saints and the Virgin Mary, as in these verses from three different milking songs:

> Come, Brendan, from the ocean,
> Come, Ternan, most potent of men,
> Come, Michael valiant, down
> And propitiate to me the cow of my joy.
>
> The charm placed of Mary of light,
> Early and late going to and from home,

The herdsman Patrick and the milkmaid Bride,
Be saining you and saving you and shielding
  you.

Come, Mary, and milk my cow,
Come, Bride, and encompass her,
Come, Columba the benign,
And twine thine arms around my cow.[8]

What is striking here is the sense of how close the
saints are. Like Mary and the angels, they are available
for mundane work in the milking parlour. This sense
that the hosts of heaven inhabit this world as well as
the next even extends to Christ and the Apostles, who
are portrayed in these beautiful verses as companions
in the boat:

Who are they on the tiller of my rudder,
  Giving speed to my east bound barge?
Peter and Paul and John the beloved,
  Three to whom laud and obeisance are due.

Who are the group near to my helm?
  Peter and Paul and John the Baptist;
Christ is sitting on my helm,
  Making guidance to the wind from the
    south.[9]

This sense of the presence of the saints and the
thinness of the veil dividing this world from the next

is also a marked feature of Welsh Christian poetry right up to our own times. Here is how Gwenallt, the great Welsh poet who lived from 1899 to 1968, began his poem in praise of St David:

> There is no border between two worlds in the
>   Church,
> The Church militant on earth
> Is one with the Church Triumphant in heaven,
> And the saints are in this Church, which is two
>   in one.
> They come to worship with us, our small
>   congregation
> The Saints who built Wales on the foundation
> Of the Crib, the Cross and the Empty Tomb.
> And they go out as before to travel their old
>   ways,
> And to earth the Gospel in Wales.

This poem, which was written in the late 1940s, goes on to portray David not as some long dead figure from the remote and distant rural past, but as one who stands alongside the workers in Wales' two great twentieth-century industries:

> He went down into the pit with the coal
>   miners
> And shone his lamp on the coal face.
> He put on the goggles of the steel worker,
> And the short grey overall.[10]

A similar sense of the continuing living presence of the early Welsh saints, and (in his words) of 'keeping house amidst a cloud of witnesses', infuses the writing of Waldo Williams, brought up a Baptist and in later life a Quaker. One of his poems recalls an incident during the First World War when with his parents, his brother and sisters, he went out into the fields one winter's night to hear the bells of the nearby village ringing in the New Year, and had a clear vision of St Tysilio, a member of the princely house of the kingdom of Powys who had renounced his royal rights to follow the monastic way. In another later poem, written as a hymn for congregational singing in 1959, Williams writes about St Brynach, an Irish saint associated with the foundation of churches on the north Pembrokeshire coast, especially that at Nevern. Donald Allchin comments that in the hymn Waldo Williams speaks 'of the restoration of kinship between earth and heaven to which the life of the saint bears witness. This he believes to be as true for us now as it was then, not least through the interweaving of Brynach's prayers with ours.'[11]

> Lord, shepherd of the ages of the earth,
>   Awakener of the grey mornings of our land,
> Your saints stand in glory,
>   Over and around the places where we dwell.
> You have given to us on the wasteland of time
>   The light of an immortal hour,

You have rekindled in our spirit
   The ancient kinship of earth and heaven.

You gave Brynach to us as a guardian,
   He raised the cross above the waves,
The storm of love on Golgotha
   Established peace in his heart;
Brynach, Irishman, look on us,
   Let our prayers flow together with yours
So that the strong walls may be raised
   Above the tempests of this world's sea.[12]

Saints are not much in vogue in contemporary Christianity. In our egalitarian culture it goes against the grain to say that some are more holy than others. Creating and celebrating saints in the Church seems to give us a two-tier model of Christianity where some are on a super-fast track to heaven. Saint-making is also suspect in Protestant eyes for interposing intermediaries into what should be a direct relationship between the individual believer and God, and for fostering cults based on superstition and relic-worship which belong more properly to pagan religion than to the Christian faith. This is, of course, why the veneration and remembrance of saints largely disappeared in Great Britain at the

Reformation. Saints have crept back a little into popular favour since then, not least as brand names for commodities ranging from processed cheese to underwear, but they still occupy a much less prominent role in both the religious and folk culture of Britain and North America than they do in Ireland and the Catholic countries of Continental Europe and Latin America.

We are right to be cynical about the way that saints have been used and abused in the history of the Christian Church. All too often their cults were largely driven by ecclesiastical power politics and they became weapons, or victims, in a propaganda war between competing ecclesiastical centres or secular power blocks. As we have seen, this was certainly the case with the cults which developed around the Celtic saints of Scotland, Ireland, Wales, Northumbria and Cornwall between the seventh and the fourteenth centuries. Yet for all the hagiographical spin-doctoring and image-making that surrounded them, the cults of the Celtic saints were rooted in a genuine popular affection and admiration for especially holy and exemplary lives. They point to the deep-seated human need for heroes, role models and figures of transparent goodness who can be revered and respected. This need is just as great now as it was in the Middle Ages – indeed it is perhaps all the greater now, when there is so much shabby tawdriness and selfish go-getting.

The most conspicuous demonstration of our

contemporary craving for saints was, of course, the public reaction that followed the death of Diana, Princess of Wales on 31 August 1997. The scenes around the London palaces resembled nothing so much as medieval saints' shrines, piled high with flowers and other votive offerings. Diana's virtual canonisation in death by both popular opinion and the media was a process that resembled the cults of the Celtic saints in a number of ways, although it was notably more instant and immediate. Like Patrick, the vulnerability and ambiguity which she had displayed and talked about in life was transformed in death into an aura of superhuman sanctity. Yet at the same time her very vulnerability and brokenness contributed to her sanctity, making her in a special way the patron saint of the marginalised and dispossessed – the gay men, the Aids victims, the Afro-Caribbeans and Asians who were to be found in disproportionate numbers among those lining up to sign the condolence books and lay flowers at the royal palaces. Like Columba, she became the posthumous victim of political and media manipulation and was taken up in death as both icon and superstar. Yet for all the consumerist and show-business hype that promoted her image in death, as it had in life, she was widely hailed as a saint by thousands of ordinary people. This came home to me when I read through the messages of condolence written in the week following her death in the books provided for the purpose in Glasgow City Chambers. The overwhelming theme of these messages, the majority of them in youthful and relatively unlettered hands, was of Diana's sanctity (the term 'Saint Diana' was used very frequently) and her passage to heaven.

The extraordinary outburst of public grief which followed Diana's death and the processes by which she was turned into a saint have been analysed in a number of extremely interesting academic studies.[13] It is clear that the impact of her death and the mourning which followed had a deeply cathartic power, allowing many people to release and express long pent-up feelings of grief and anxiety and enabling others to re-establish long-lost connections with faith communities, church worship and prayer. In his book, *Diana: Icon and Sacrifice*, Ted Harrison describes the case of a woman who went to church for the first time in many years on the Sunday that Diana died and has since prayed every day. He also points out that in the three months following Diana's death there was a 50 per cent reduction in admissions to psychiatric clinics and hospitals, and quotes the views of three medical practitioners on the therapeutic benefits in terms of relieving stress, depression and anxiety which came about as a result of people crying and unleashing their emotions.[14]

In this respect, Diana, like the Celtic saints, displayed healing powers in death as in life. The fact that she died in the same week as Mother Teresa of Calcutta encouraged comparisons between these two women as the outstanding saints of the late twentieth century. Italian Roman Catholics placed painted figures of Diana alongside shepherds and wise men in their Christmas cribs and even made statues of her modelled on the familiar image of the Madonna. In many ways Diana's 'canonisation' after death betokened the stirring of latent spiritual and ethical values as well as sentimentalism and hysteria. It can be seen as a protest against the whole debunking, anti-heroic tendency of contemporary culture and as a sign of the desperate desire to have figures to revere and admire. Yet in other respects Diana's sainthood was altogether different from that of Mother Teresa and those who go through the conventional canonisation process. She has been well described as the first post-modern saint, her beatitude constructed in a multiplicity of different narratives – as feminist icon, symbol of maternal love or single motherhood, nationalist heroine, sign of hope for the suffering and dispossesed, unifying point of identification for minority groups – and expressed in terms of desire.[15] She was also the first royal icon raised on and sustained by the pop culture. There is a profound ambiguity between her saintliness and her status as pop superstar. Was she mourned as a saint or a celebrity? Indeed, did the cult that followed her death betoken the triumph of new wholly secular concept of sainthood in which celebrity and star quality had altogether eclipsed any concept of the sacred?

There is no doubt that we live in a culture where a huge premium is put on celebrity. The media's fickle fascination with building up and destroying reputations, the relentless commercial pressure constantly to create new fads and crazes, the primacy of pop music and sport in popular culture, the heavy emphasis on youth and innovation and the short attention spans and jaded appetites bred of the soundbite/channel-hopping mentality combine to give us an ever-changing array of iconic superstars, here today and gone tomorrow, who provide the young in particular with their role models and exemplars. When in 1997 a representative national sample of 9-to-13-year-olds were asked which famous person they most admired, the top answers were Geri of the Spice Girls, Leonardo DiCaprio and Tom Cruise. Today the names would be different but they would be similarly drawn exclusively from the world of entertainment. No one outside the ranks of show business and sport appeared anywhere in these youthful lists of heroes and heroines.

The devotion which these contemporary icons inspire is strongly reminiscent of that once given to Celtic saints. I became aware of this during the *floruit* of the cult of the Spice Girls. There was a period for about nine months during 1997 when it was almost impossible to go into the bedroom of a child aged between nine and twelve without finding a poster of the pouting, scantily clad fivesome grinning down from the wall. It was often in exactly the spot above the bed where once there might have been in Protestant homes an improving biblical text and in

Catholic homes a crucifix or picture of the Virgin. The parallel was even more marked when for the Christmas market standing figures of Geri, Victoria, Emma and the two Mels (whose names always struck me as ideal for Cornish saints) came out looking for all the world like those plaster casts of saints that still grace souvenir shops at major Catholic shrines.

A recent exhibition at the Tate Gallery in Liverpool entitled 'Heaven: An Exhibition that will Break Your Heart' explored how cults based on the adoration of pop singers, royalty and fashion models are replacing the traditional subjects of Christian worship. It included a statue of Lady Diana as the Madonna, a sweatcloth of Elvis Presley designed to emulate the Turin shroud and mugs modelled on Marilyn Monroe's breasts. The curator noted that icons like Presley, Monroe and Princess Diana 'are being cherished as sacred figures. The ritual accompanying stars and celebrities or the booming market of fan articles is almost identical to the business of saints' relics.' The publicity material for the exhibition made an even more explicit connection:

> Religious imagery and ritual is no longer contained within a traditional, sacred place. Celebrities, supermodels and pop stars are now idolised and adored as once were saints and angels. A tropical beach resort or a fashionable shopping mall has become, for many, a vision of 'paradise'. We worship at the graves of the

famous, at rock concerts and fashion shows.
The concept of the sublime, of the awe-
inspiring and the perfect, has changed drastically in recent decades, a change reflected in
contemporary art.[16]

On the whole, religious leaders asked for their
comments on this exhibition by the press were negative and used words like offensive and blasphemous.
Yet in some ways the Church must take some of the
blame for the fact that these secular icons have
stepped into the vacuum created by the large-scale
withdrawal of saints from popular Christianity. The
popular appetite for saints and the human need for
figures to look up to have not gone away. They have
shifted to new secular icons thanks predominantly to
the power of certain commercial interests and
marketing hype but also because of the Church's lack
of interest in and positive distaste for this area.
We urgently need to identify and promote both
historical and contemporary figures who can provide
inspiration, act as role models and help to promote
the world-challenging values of Christianity in our
celebrity-conscious and star-struck culture. We need
especially to fill children's minds with stories of
saints and heroes. We may cynically sneer at hymns
which begin 'O Son of Man, our hero strong and ten-
der', or 'When a knight won his spurs in the stories
of old', but they at least address the appetite among
young people for people to look up to and emulate.

If we withdraw them and put nothing in their place, we leave the media and advertising agencies a free rein and a monopoly on the hearts and minds of the young.

Personal example and life stories generally have a more direct and lasting effect on people than improving homilies and abstract theorising. Basil Hume rightly observed that 'Saints from all ages have something to say to us. Their lives speak eloquently of God. We can be more touched by contact with holy people than by any number of sermons.'[17] The Vatican is right to be putting Mother Teresa on a first track to canonisation. The present pope is right to be making more saints than any of his recent predecessors. Westminster Abbey is to be applauded for placing statues of ten twentieth-century martyrs, including Martin Luther King, Dietrich Bonhoeffer and Oscar Romero, in niches above the great west door. Saints speak to us directly through the power of their stories and personalities where theological jargon and sermonising often only serve to turn us off. Their ranks are not, of course, confined to those officially canonised by the Church or widely recognised as famous martyrs. There are many saints living in our midst whose quiet faith and courage in the face of adversity put them firmly in the ranks of the saints even though they would never themselves claim that title. These are the kind of people featured in the excellent flagship BBC Television religious programme *Songs of Praise*, or more precisely in those editions of the programme which still come from real communities and do not rely on showbiz stars and gimmicky locations. Even now, when that programme like so many others has largely succumbed to the celebrity cult, one still happens across a *Songs of Praise* which visits an ordinary place and talks to 'ordinary' people about their faith and their life stories. They turn out to be extraordinary people, whose stories make easily the most inspiring and memorable part of the week's viewing. We need to develop and promote more programmes which celebrate the saints in our midst.

In one sense, celebrating the saints in our midst means our being less egalitarian and recognising that there are individuals of outstanding personal holiness. These same individuals are invariably also extremely modest and self-effacing. Indeed, they have those qualities of humility combined with piety which characterised Columba and Patrick. The vast majority of them will never in any official sense be recognised as saints of the Church. Yet they perform in their quiet and unassuming way what is surely the vital role of saints, reflecting Christ in their lives in a particularly intense and moving way and pointing us to him.

In Celtic Christianity, as we have seen, sainthood was often associated with leadership. This is another dimension which we badly need to recover. On the whole, those whom I have just identified as saints today are very far from positions of authority and would often shy away from leadership roles. Yet some of them may be precisely the people we need to lead churches and other institutions and groups. The model of leadership which Celtic Christianity has given us is one rooted in spiritual authority where natural qualities of leadership, often associated with high birth and breeding, combine with humility and manifest integrity to produce a spiritual authority which is widely recognised and respected. In my book on Columba, I reflected that what he tells us about leadership is perhaps his most important and difficult message for us today. It was because his contemporaries acknowledged his saintliness and were ready to follow his leadership that he was able to do all that he did for Christ. Were he to come back today, I suspect that he would be put down by colleagues jealous of his advantages of birth and his evident talents, hounded by tabloid journalists determined to dig out the dirt in his past, and squashed by committees anxious to maintain the status quo and preserve a quiet life. The modern Church has opted to be run by management structures rather than led by saints. We prefer setting up working parties to following a prophet.

The issue of leadership is an extraordinarily confused one in the contemporary Church. Authority in the Celtic church was personal rather than institutional. Most modern churches are increasingly setting up complex institutional structures in an effort to diffuse and decentralise authority. There are good reasons for doing so. The dangers of allowing charismatic leaders a power and influence in the Church unfettered by institutional checks and balances were all too clearly shown in the scandal involving the Sheffield Nine O'Clock service. Yet in our quest for accountability, decentralisation, corporate management and democratic participation, have we left any room for leadership? No doubt Columba had a fiercely autocratic side and rubbed some people up the wrong way. Yet ultimately he achieved what he did because he was recognised as a leader and people were prepared to follow him, just as five hundred years earlier people had been prepared to follow Jesus of Nazareth. Like Jesus, Columba spoke as one having authority.

We must not be frightened of personal leadership in the Church or in other areas. Its proper exercise is an extremely important Christian vocation. Cultivating, nurturing and affirming qualities of leadership is a deeply worthwhile and deeply Christian task. It was an important element in the life of the Celtic monastery. It is both significant and encouraging that the spiritual roots and dimension of leadership are now once again being explored in a monastic context and offered to the wider world of business and administration. Both Douai Abbey in Berkshire and Ampleforth Abbey in North Yorkshire have recently started running courses on leadership for businessmen based on the application of the Rule of St Benedict to modern management. An article by

the *Daily Telegraph*'s religious correspondent, Victoria
Combe, under the headline 'How businessmen can
learn from a sixth century saint', listed several 'top
tips for top managers' which she had gleaned from
one of the Ampleforth courses. They include the
importance of keeping everyone occupied and
recognising that 'idleness is the enemy of the soul',
managing things 'so that the strong may have ideals
to inspire them and the weak may not be frightened',
recognising that the manager's goal must be 'profit
for the monks, not pre-eminence for himself', and
getting the whole community together and personally explaining the agenda when any business of
importance is to be considered.[18]

In another significant recent initiative, more
directly inspired by the example of Celtic
Christianity, Norman Drummond has set up the
Columba 1400 project on the isle of Skye. This aims
to provide a community and international leadership
centre located in the remote hamlet of Staffin which
will house residential courses for decision-makers
in the professions, the public sector and business,
and for young people from both advantaged and
disadvantaged backgrounds. While the accent is on
leadership-training through team-building exercises,
communication skills, management development
and executive training, the centre will also take on
several other roles appropriate to a modern Celtic
monasterium by providing a wide range of facilities for
the local community, including internet access, an

all-day café, a homework study area, a games room and quiet areas which will be used for regular morning and evening meditation.

There is another important respect in which the *monasterium* model may provide a more appropriate style of leadership for the Church today than those favoured in many long-established denominations. It was exemplified in the person of Basil Hume, the Abbot of Ampleforth who went on to become Cardinal Archbishop of Westminster and leader of the Roman Catholic Church in England and Wales. I was struck with what the *Tablet* said about him after his death in June 1999:

> He came not from the Venerable English College or diocesan seminary tradition, which has been the traditional background of English and Welsh bishops, but from the different world of monasticism with a dynamic of its own. One of its greatest contributions, largely through his influence, has been to change the temper of English Catholicism from a tendency to judge and exclude to a desire to embrace and include. He built bridges rather than burned them.[19]

This is the kind of leadership that today's churches need. The monastic abbot has the humility and sanctity of the monk but also the authority of one who commands obedience and who is firm and disciplined. These were the qualities that shone

through the great Celtic monk bishops like Aidan,
Ninian and David. Their authority was rooted in their
monastic obedience and in their position in community. One of the most widely respected and effective
bishops in the Episcopal Church of the United States
is a monastic, Bishop M. Thomas Shaw of
Massachusetts, who draws his inspiration from St
David. Leadership is a complex amalgam of natural
authority, charisma, and the legacy of birth and
breeding. We should not neglect this last element in
our egalitarian culture. Basil Hume undoubtedly
derived some of his leadership quality from his
upper middle-class birth and breeding. So did George
MacLeod and many other church leaders of recent
times. Addressing a conference in 1895 on the Celtic
inheritance of the Scottish church, James Cooper,
church historian, ecumenist and Celtophile, argued
that acting in the spirit of Columba, the modern
Church of Scotland should draw more on those of
high rank and noble birth and use 'the gifted sons
of our nobles and chiefs' to provide both church
leaders and lay assistants to assist parish clergy.[20] A
hundred years on, the churches are perhaps in even
more need of a reminder to identify and value
those in their own ranks who have both natural and
inherited leadership qualities and not be quite so
self-consciously and self-righteously egalitarian in
this area.

The Celtic saints, as we have seen, were even more
important in death than in life. They were seen as

belonging to that great company of heaven that encompass and surround us on earth. Their continuing protective power and efficacy and their lively presence beyond the grave did much to break down the fear and barrier of death and to point to the thinness of the veil that separates this world from the next. Greater attachment to the doctrine of the Communion of Saints would help us today to make death less of a taboo subject and to help people express their feelings of grief at the loss of loved ones. The outburst of public mourning that followed the death of Diana, Princess of Wales, enabled many people to express grief that they had long bottled up for departed friends and family . This was very evident from the messages of condolence that I looked at in Glasgow where again and again Diana's death was linked to the death of a much loved relative or friend. They also indicated a huge urge to communicate with the dead. Diana was seen as a go-between who could take messages of love and remembrance to departed loved ones.

At present, the churches are not meeting people in their desire to communicate with the dead and to preserve a lively reminder of them. As a result we have a mushrooming of interest in spiritualism, ouija boards and mediums and an obsession with ghosts and ghouls, vampires and the undead. People are turning to these esoteric and often dangerous aspects of the occult because the Church seems to offer them so little contact with the dead. We need to reconnect with the hosts of heaven and the crowd of witnesses that surround us. We should not be afraid of praying for the dead. In the Irish church such prayers were seen as a very important aspect of care for the dead. This is best handled through a revived doctrine of the Communion of Saints, seen in terms of the continuing and close presence of those who have departed from this life, not just the great figures canonised by the Church but those we have known and loved and learned from in our own family and friends.

This vivid sense of the reality of the Communion of Saints is superbly expressed in a way that is both pastorally very helpful to the bereaved and also quite acceptable to Protestant sensibilities in one of the great prayers crafted by George MacLeod. It is entitled 'A Veil Thin as Gossamer':

> Be Thou, triune God, in the midst of us as we give thanks for those who have gone from the sight of earthly eyes. They, in Thy nearer presence, still worship with us in the mystery of the one family in heaven and on earth.
>
> We remember those whom Thou didst call to high office, as the world counts high. They bore the agony of great decisions and laboured to fashion the Ark of the Covenant nearer to Thy design.
>
> We remember those who, little recognised in

the sight of men, bore the heat and burden of
the unrecorded day. They served serene because
they knew Thou hadst made them priests and
kings, and now shine as the stars forever.

If it be Thy holy will, tell them how we love
them, and how we miss them, and how we
long for the day when we shall meet with
them again.

God of all comfort, we lift into Thine immediate care those recently bereaved, who sometimes in the night time cry 'would God it were
morning', and in the morning cry 'would God
it were night'. Bereft of their dear ones, too
often they are bereft also of the familiar scenes
where happiness once reigned.

Lift from their eyes the too distant vision of
the resurrection at the last day. Alert them to
hear the voice of Jesus saying 'I AM
Resurrection and I AM Life': that they may
believe this.

Strengthen them to go on in loving service of
all Thy children. Thus shall they have communion with Thee and, in Thee, with their beloved.
Thus shall they come to know, in themselves,
that there is no death and that only a veil
divides, thin as gossamer.[21]

A lively doctrine of the Communion of Saints brings us into contact with our roots and traditions. This is a considerable benefit in an age like ours where so many are rootless and alienated. The Communion of Saints links us to the Church universal throughout the world and throughout history, enabling us to locate ourselves in a great tradition which stretches back 2,000 years and forwards into eternity. It provides, in T. S. Eliot's words, 'the point of intersection of the timeless with time'. It enables us, as Edward Bickersteth so splendidly put it in the last verse of his hymn 'For my sake, and the Gospel's, go and tell redemption's story', to raise our anthems of praise 'in concert with the holy dead'. It enables us to recall and to offer thanksgiving for 'the saints who before us have found their reward', as W. H. Draper did in his great hymn for the dedication of a church entitled 'In remembrance of past worshippers'. It lets us affirm with William Walsham How:

> O blest communion! fellowship divine!
> We feebly struggle, they in glory shine;
> Yet all are one in thee, for all are thine.

Charles Wesley felt that it was especially through singing hymns and psalms left by former generations that we gain our sense of the Communion of Saints and the great continuity and tradition of Christian worship and witness through the ages. Certainly that for me is the most vivid way of connecting with the great tradition. But as well as linking us with the great universal tradition of prayer and praise throughout the ages, saints also give a particular sense of local identity and place. This is particularly true of the Celtic saints whose cults, as we have seen, were much more localised and rooted in particular places than those of the Catholic Continental saints. There has been a welcome recovery of interest in sacred places in our age, many of which are tied to Celtic saints. Often they provide the inspiration for significant expressions of contemporary Christian witness, like the healing ministry at Pennant Melangell in mid-Wales, the pilgrimage up Croagh Patrick in western Ireland and the trail to St Fergus' well at Glamis in Eastern Scotland restored by un-employed youngsters. Celtic saints remain an important focus for local customs and identity at a time when both are in danger of disappearing.

We need to recover the sense of the saints as a live-ly presence, a cloud of witnesses that though unseen surrounds and enfolds us. Having a much livelier sense of the doctrine of the Communion of Saints does not mean dwelling in a morbid way on the departed and their relics but it does mean acknow-ledging the closeness of the dead, affirming the doctrine of resurrection and celebrating the sacramental value of both place and tradition. Ultimately saints are vital because, in the words of David Adam, a church without saints is a church without heaven. Saints are, indeed, in a very real sense colonists of heaven, going before us in the faith, pointing us to the reality of resurrection and the world to come, binding us in the one body of the Church, militant here on earth and triumphant in heaven. Their nearness reminds us of the thinness of the veil of gossamer that divides this world from the next. Their encompassing presence and protection enables us to run with patience the race that is set before us.

6

Pilgrimage

After ten years of exploring Celtic Christianity in
all sorts of moods – with the enthusiasm of the
convert, the scepticism of the scholar, the faith of
the believer, the misty eyes of the romantic and the
hard-headed detachment of the academic – I remain
convinced of one thing: that pilgrimage is its single
most important and distinctive theme. It provided
the subject matter for the concluding chapters of
both *The Celtic Way* and *Columba*, as it does also for this
book. Pilgrimage has, indeed, been the one constant
in my own peregrinations around and along the
Celtic way – in so far as one can describe as a
constant what is rather a perpetual moving on,
venturing out into unknown territory and meeting
new fellow-travellers along the way.

The theme of pilgrimage dominates Celtic Christianity at both the literal and the symbolic level. If I was ever to make a film about the Christian life of the British Isles in the period between the departure of the Romans and the coming of the Normans I would be tempted to title it 'monks on the move'. The lives of the saints and other early sources are full of accounts of the constant criss-crossing of sea ways and overland routes by monks going on preaching and pastoral tours or setting out to found monastic communities and plant new colonies of heaven. Unlike their Benedictine counterparts, Irish monks did not take a vow of stability to their mother house. Perhaps it was recognised as a non-starter, given the Celtic wanderlust. Maybe there was also a conscious echo of the spirit of perpetual exile and wandering which animated the desert fathers and which was emulated by those many Celtic saints who sought out their own desert places of resurrection, and in so doing made Dysserth, Dysart and Diseart popular place names in Wales, Scotland and Ireland.

In symbolic terms, pilgrimage was a favourite metaphor to express the Celtic emphasis on the dynamic character of Christian faith. It is there in the sermons of Columbanus which describe the Christian life as a journey and this earth as a way and not a resting place or destination. The same message is conveyed in artistic terms in the endlessly intertwining and never-ending motif of the Celtic knot which I analysed in *The Celtic Way* and in the cantillation of the antiphons in honour of Columba in the Inchcolm Antiphoner with their greater sense of movement and freedom than the more static, earthbound tones of Gregorian chant. Pilgrim imagery features prominently in Irish, Welsh and Hebridean prayers and poetry. It is a dominant motif in the Irish penitentials and in the sacramental offices of the early Irish and Scottish church with their emphasis on providing spiritual food for those on life's journey and on the journey into death. Pilgrimage is of course central to the concept which gives this book its title and underlying theme. If Christians are indeed colonists of heaven on earth, then they are in a very real sense pilgrims in a land that is at once both barren and alien and yet also shot through with sacramental potential and possibility.

It is important to be clear that the Celtic Christian understanding of pilgrimage was very different from the view generally held in the Middle Ages. In this later understanding, which to a large extent remains the conventional modern view, pilgrimage involves a purposeful journey to a particular holy place in order to gain a special spiritual buzz or 'high'. The early Irish monks had little time for this approach, as a verse attributed to one of them makes clear:

Who to Rome goes
Much labour, little profit knows;

For God, on earth though long you have
  sought him,
You'll miss at Rome unless you've brought
  him.[1]

This same sentiment is well expressed in an imagined
conversation between the old monk, Ruadh, and his
soul friend, the young monk, Aidan, who is about to
go off to Byzantium to present the emperor with the
Book of Kells in one of Stephen Lawhead's modern
novels about Celtic Christianity in its 'golden age':
'Remember, Aidan. Never doubt in the darkness that
which you believed in the light. Also, this: unless the
pilgrim carry with him the thing he seeks, he will
not find it when he arrives.'[2] For the Irish monks,
pilgrimage was first and foremost an inner state of
mind expressed in outward terms in a life of physical exile and journeying. Few expressed both the
inner and the outer aspects of pilgrimage better than
Columbanus, who travelled across Europe founding
monasteries and preached sermons pointing to the
provisional and transitory nature of human life and
the importance of seeing it as a pilgrim's way:

> What then are you, human life? You are the
> roadway of mortals, not their life, beginning
> from sin, enduring up till death . . . so you are
> the way to life, not life; for you are a real way,
> but not an open one, long for some, short for
> others, broad for some, narrow for others,

joyful for some, sad for others, for all alike
hasting and irrevocable. A way is what you are,
a way, but you are not manifest to all; for many
see you, and few understand you to be a way;
for on a roadway none dwells but walks, that
those who walk upon the way may dwell in
their homeland.[3]

This understanding of pilgrimage was based on
the premise that Christians are first and foremost
colonists of heaven. It is the view of pilgrimage that
essentially informed both the New Testament and
early Church, a view later replaced by the medieval
concept (of purposeful journeying to a holy place in
order to procure spiritual benefit) which has unfortunately remained dominant up to our own times.
Columbanus' words echo the famous passage in
Hebrews 11:13–16 which speaks of Christians as
strangers and exiles on earth seeking a homeland in
that better country which is heaven. This notion that
Christians have their dwelling on earth but belong as
citizens in heaven was widely held throughout the
early Church.

Pilgrimage, conceived in this radical and un-
comfortable way, was a key feature of Irish monastic
life, with its emphasis on costly witness and discipline. Many monks expressed their discipleship by
becoming *peregrini pro Christo* (pilgrims for Christ) and
following the path of white martyrdom, perpetually
exiling themselves from the pleasures, distractions

and attachments of the world and especially of home and family. This understanding of pilgrimage, so clearly expressed in Columbanus' sermons, may well have inspired Columba's decision to quit his beloved Ireland, and certainly informs the well-known story that he did not stop and settle until he reached a place from which he could no longer see his homeland. It went with a commitment to live lightly to the world and avoid its values of acquisitiveness and accumulating material possessions (even to this day there is no Irish word to correspond with the English term 'possessions'). In a beautiful phrase, the Irish monks spoke of themselves living as *hospites mundi*, or guests of the world. *Peregrinatio* was seen as a way of living in imitation of Christ and moving towards Christian perfection. In the words of the Old Irish Penitential, 'As for him who desires to reach the pitch of perfectness, he distributes all he has to the poor and needy and goes on pilgrimage or lives in destitution in a communal church until he goes to Heaven.'[4]

The search by monks for their places of resurrection forms a major theme in the lives of the Celtic saints. It was apparently to secure a safe passage for a group of Iona monks led by Cormac who had set off into the seas north of the Scottish mainland that Columba visited the court of the Pictish King Brude near Inverness. There he told the sub-king of the Orkneys, where the monks seem to have ended up, that 'some of our people have recently gone out desiring to find a desert place in the sea that cannot be crossed'.[5] Another story in Adamnan's life of Columba makes clear that in the monastic context pilgrimage was not simply something to be engaged in on a whim or out of wanderlust but only with the express sanction and permission of the abbot. It again concerns Cormac, 'a truly holy man who laboured three times on the ocean in search of a place of retreat yet found none', about whom Columba prophesies:

> Today again Cormac, desiring to find a desert, begins his voyage from the district that is called Eirros domno, lying beyond the River Mod. But this time also he will not find what he seeks; and for no other fault on his part than that he has improperly taken with him as a companion on his voyage a man who, being the monk of a religious abbot, has departed without the abbot's consent.[6]

Pilgrimage was often prescribed as a penance or punishment. The penitential associated with Columbanus decreed that anyone who commited murder after becoming a monk 'shall die unto the world with *peregrinatione perenni*'. According to some accounts, a similar kind of banishment rather than a voluntary exile may have lain behind Columba's departure from Ireland to Iona. Whether voluntary or enforced, *peregrinatio* was viewed as a risky and dangerous enterprise which involved leaving the security of the monastery and journeying into the unknown, often by launching off from the shore in a coracle and venturing into the perilous deep. In both literal and symbolic terms it meant casting off the security of dry land and trusting yourself utterly to God. Small islands in inhospitable seas, like Eileach an Naoimh and the Gavellochs in the Firth of Lorne and Skellig Michael off the south coast of Ireland, were especially sought after as places of pilgrimage. Yet for all its lonely isolation and painful penitential character, pilgrimage, like other aspects of Celtic Christianity, was also a matter of balance and rhythm. In common with other monks, Columba and Cuthbert alternated between periods of intense activity running their busy monastic *familia* and weeks or months of solitary withdrawal on their respective island retreats of Hinba and Farne island. There was a deeper sense in which a life of inner as well as outward pilgrimage was seen as having an essential rhythm and harmony. 'Every day you depart and every day you return' preached Columbanus in a sermon about human life.[7]

As practised by the Irish monks, pilgrimage was an intensely physical activity. Like their long hours spent with arms outstretched in the cross vigil, standing in the sea reciting the psalms or genuflecting before the altar, it engaged the body as much as the soul or the intellect in the business of Christian worship and discipleship. This important dimension of Celtic Christianity has been somewhat overlooked in its

current rather 'bookish' revival. It put a high
premium on those now sadly rather maligned values
of muscular Christianity and Christian manliness. Ray
Simpson, one of the few leading figures in the
contemporary revival who has highlighted this
aspect, suggests that Celtic Christianity is particularly
well equipped to speak to the modern crisis of male
identity, highlighted in books like *Iron John* and
movements like the Promise Keepers. He points out
that it is essentially (although not exclusively) manly,
inheriting and affirming from pre-Christian Celtic
society the male image of warrior and hunter. This
element of Christian manliness is very clearly present
in the image of the pilgrim. An Irish boat song
associated with Columbanus and possibly sung by his
monks as they rowed up the Rhine in 610 pre-echoes
the great nineteenth-century pilgrim hymn 'Through
the night of doubt and sorrow', with its wonderful-
ly evocative (and now often sadly emasculated) line
'brother clasps the hand of brother'. In Simpson's
words, it 'captures a manhood shorn of romantic
frills that was honed in the hard tasks instilled by
their Master, Christ'.[8]

> The tempests howl, the storms dismay,
> But manly strength can win the day.
> Heave, lads, and let the echoes ring.
>
> For clouds and squalls will soon pass on,
> And victory lie with work well done.
> Heave, lads, and let the echoes ring.

Hold fast! Survive! And all is well,
God sent you worse. He'll calm this swell.
Heave, lads, and let the echoes ring.

So Satan acts to tire the brain,
And by temptation souls are slain.
Think, lads, of Christ, and echo him.

The king of virtues vowed a prize,
For him who wins, for him who tries.
Think, lads, of Christ, and echo him.[9]

For us today, pilgrimage often carries the connotation of walking together with others, including those from different denominational and theological perspectives and even, perhaps, of different faiths. How far was this idea embedded in the Celtic Christian notion of pilgrimage? This is a difficult and controversial area. There was, of course, no real denominational agenda or division in pre-Reformation British Christianity. The opposition between the so-called Celtic and Roman churches which has been made so much of by certain historians almost certainly reflects post-Reformation conceptions and distorts the sense of oneness and universality in earlier British Christianity. How far early Celtic Christians walked alongside pagans and were open to pre-Christian and other traditions is a vexed question. There is as at least as much evidence of confrontation as of syncretism and co-operation.

Recent studies have suggested that Anglo-Saxon Christians may, in fact, have been very much more tolerant of and open to pagans than their Celtic cousins. It was, after all, the much-maligned Augustine who was specifically charged by Pope Gregory on the eve of his 'Roman' mission to England in 597 not to destroy heathen shrines nor force people to give up their sacrifices, but rather to work with existing beliefs and rituals and bring them into the Christian economy of salvation. Paul Cavill has recently argued that Anglo-Saxon Christianity was intensely pragmatic, recognising the importance of habit and working with existing local traditions, although he strongly rejects the notion that it was syncretistic. Celtic Christianity he sees as much more dualistic and confrontational, radically separating the sacred and secular, pagan and Christian, and being more concerned with conversion than integration. I suspect that he may well be right and that in respect of the whole area of inculturation, as in other fields, we should probably be giving more credit to the rather despised Anglo-Saxons and less to the all-popular Celts.[10]

One pilgrim theme does seem to link pre- and post-Christian Celtic literature. This is the motif of fantastic journeys and wanderings which provides the subject matter of two distinctive genres in pre-Christian Celtic mythology, the *immrama* (tales of voyage) and the *echtrai* which deal specifically with adventures to the other world. Celtic Christianity also has its tales of fantastic journeys, most famously in the *Navigatio Sancti Brendani* (*Voyage of St Brendan*) which probably dates from the ninth or early tenth century but may be of earlier provenance. This epic story, which may either echo or provide a model for the mythological *Voyage of Braan*, tells of St Brendan's seven-year journeyings around the islands of the remote western seas, including the island of women and the island of birds. At one level, it can be interpreted as a journey to the promised land and an allegory of the Christian life in the style of John Bunyan's *Pilgrim's Progress*. Brendan's quest to find the land promised to the saints brings him at last to the banks of a great river too broad and deep to cross. Here a young man tells him that God has kept him wandering for so long to show him the mysteries of the ocean, and that the promised land will only be revealed in God's good time after much persecution and tribulation. Jonathan Wooding, who has done much academic study on the *Navigatio*, suggests that it may, in fact, provide an elaborate metaphor for the monastic life with its discipline, its emphasis on *peregrinatio*, its sense of time elapsing and its message that 'for a monk almost the most important thing is running to stand still'.[11]

As we have already noted, the theme of pilgrimage is fundamental to understanding the Irish penitential system. Surveying various approaches to penance and confession, Hugh Connolly identifies that based on the model of pilgrimage as 'the most quintessentially Celtic'.[12] At its root, he suggests, 'is the image of life-pilgrimage and suffering. Here sin is seen as wandering from the right path, penance thus becomes re-orientation and the confessor is portrayed as a fellow-traveller, fellow-sufferer or *anamchara*.'[13] Fundamental to the Irish penitentials was an understanding of the Christian life as a progression and not as something static. Echoing Cassian's belief that 'we march forward in the love of God', they prescribed an arduous training regime of penances, fasting and vigils for the sinner so that he might grow and develop. For Columbanus, the rigours of this earthly training found their reward in heaven: 'This is in fact the training of all trainings, and at the price of present sorrow it prepares the pleasure of unending time and the delight of unending joy.'[14] In Connolly's words:

> The Celtic image of pilgrimage affords a vision
> of the Christian life wherein the individual will
> inevitably encounter suffering and sin, but
> where he has also the means, through
> penance, to cleave to that graced process,
> whereby he is freed from the un-Christ-like
> elements which impede the growth of his
> humanity into the kingdom.[15]

In this Celtic understanding of pilgrimage, the individual does not just rely on penance but is sustained and supported by soul friends, the sacraments of the Church which provide the *viaticum* or

food for the journey into the next world and, over-
whelmingly, by the prevenient grace and all-
encompassing love of God. The image of journeying
runs through much of the devotional literature of
Celtic Christianity. So too does the portrayal of God as
a travelling companion, both sharing and leading the
way, as in this early Irish hymn attributed to
Columba:

> Alone with none but thee, my God,
>   I journey on my way;
> What need I fear, when thou art near,
>   O King of night and day?
> More safe am I within thy hand,
> Than if a host did round me stand.
>
> My destined time is fixed by thee,
>   And Death doth know his hour.
> Did warriors strong around me throng,
>   They could not stay his power;
> No walls of stone can man defend
> When thou thy messenger dost send.
>
> My life I yield to thy decree,
>   And bow to thy control
> In peaceful calm, for from thine arm
>   No power can wrest my soul.
> Could earthly omens e'er appal
> A man that heeds the heavenly call!

The child of God can fear no ill,
　　His chosen dread no foe;
We leave our fate with thee, and wait
　　Thy bidding when to go.
'Tis not from chance our comfort springs,
Thou art our trust, O King of kings.[16]

Many of the Hebridean prayers collected and translated by Alexander Carmichael in the late nineteenth century similarly take up the twin themes of human journeying and God's enfolding love, now more likely to be specifically associated with the person of Christ. This one was recited by Ann Mackinnon, a crofter on the island of Coll:

The Gospel of the God of life
To shelter thee, to aid thee,
Yea, the Gospel of beloved Christ
The holy Gospel of the Lord;

To keep thee from all malice,
From every dole and dolour;
To keep thee from all spite,
From evil eye and anguish.

Thou shalt travel thither, thou shalt travel
　hither,
Thou shalt travel hill and headland,
Thou shalt travel down, thou shalt travel up,
Thou shalt travel ocean and narrow.

Christ Himself is shepherd over thee,
Enfolding thee on every side;
He will not forsake thee hand or foot,
Nor let evil come anigh thee.[17]

The revival of pilgrimage has been one of the most striking and surprising religious movements of recent years. Inspired in part by the increasing enthusiasm for ecumenical ventures, the growing yearning for spirituality and a new interest in sacred places, it has brought thousands of people from different Christian denominations together as pilgrims to share a physical and spiritual journey lasting anything from a few hours to several weeks. A number of long-distance footpaths have been opened up in the last few years specifically so that modern pilgrims can follow in the footsteps of the Celtic saints. The old pilgrim route along the northern shores of the Solway Firth to Whithorn has been waymarked with signs bearing the distinctive logo of the Celtic cross and is the focus for an annual walk to support Christian Aid. St Cuthbert's Way is a recently opened long-distance foothpath covering the sixty-two and a half miles between Melrose and Lindisfarne. A pilgrimage to Bardsey Island off the western tip of the Llyn Peninsula in north-west Wales led by Cleadan

Mears, Bishop of Bangor, in 1992 revived another ancient Celtic tradition and the island of 20,000 saints now plays host to a steady stream of modern pilgrims who seek a week's retreat in a simple cottage without electricity, running water or sanitation.

In Ireland, a cross-border Columba trail, opened in 1997 as part of the celebrations to mark the 1400th anniversary of the saint's death, links sites in Antrim and Derry with his supposed birthplace in Donegal. Michael Rodgers, the Roman Catholic priest at Glendalough, has developed a pilgrim trail through the valley that once housed one of the largest early medieval monastic cities in order that modern-day pilgrims can 'pray following in the footsteps of St Kevin and the Celtic saints'. Many smaller-scale and more localised pilgrim routes have been developed, like the path to St Fergus' Well at Glamis, restored under the direction of Andrew Greaves. At a national level, the Sacred Land project, launched in 1997, has the avowed aim of reopening ancient pilgrimage routes throughout Britain, creating new pilgrim paths, assisting in restoring old shrines and sacred sites and fostering awareness that 'everywhere is potentially sacred, and therefore to encourage us to walk gently, for we walk on sacred ground'.[18] There are even ambitious plans to revive one of the longest and most celebrated Celtic pilgrim routes across Continental Europe. Derry Healey, a priest belonging to the missionary order of St Columbanus, is hoping to take groups of young people in the footsteps of the

saint and his followers across France, Switzerland and
Northern Italy.

These and other pilgrimage initiatives and projects
are part of a wider rediscovery of the spiritual
benefits gained when people from different backgrounds and traditions walk and talk together. By no
means all draw directly on Celtic influences and
inspiration – the annual Whitekirk to Haddington
pilgrimage in East Lothian which brings together
increasing numbers of Presbyterians, Episcopalians
and Roman Catholics is a case in point, being an
essentially modern ecumenical project, though drawing its inspiration from medieval traditions.
Common to them all, however, is that understanding
of the value of pilgrimage, as a symbol of the journey of faith as well as a physical activity, which was
so marked a feature of Celtic Christianity. It was with
this object in mind that the organisation Pilgrim
Adventure was founded in 1987 to combine the
adventure of travel 'off the beaten track' with the purpose and spirit of pilgrimage, and to demonstrate
that the Christian journey is an adventure.

Alongside this recovery of the religious dimension
of pilgrimage there has also been a more tourist-
oriented and commercially driven campaign to
market ancient Christian sites as attractive venues for
holidaymakers and day-trippers. Celtic Christian sites
have been in the van of these developments. The last
few years have seen major new visitor centres opened
at Lindisfarne, Glendalough and Fionnphort on Mull

(to introduce the story of Columba to those about to make the short ferry crossing to Iona). Whithorn now promotes itself as 'the cradle of Christianity' and an 'all-weather attraction' offering 'live archaeology' as the team excavating Ninian's monastery dig up their finds under the gaze of visitors. These and other Celtic Christian sites like Clonmacnoise are all now very much on the tourist circuit, their expanded carparks regularly filled throughout the summer by cars and coaches.

Several enterprising strategies are being employed to turn those visiting these sites from tourists into pilgrims. A series of pilgrim guides to such places as Iona, Lindisfarne, St David's and Durham attempt to show the Christian history and spiritual significance that lies behind their contemporary visitor appeal. Prayers, services and sometimes counselling opportunities are offered for those making day visits, and retreat houses provide the opportunity for people to make longer stays involving participation in regular worship, discussion groups, guided reading and spiritual direction. The Celi De programme, run from Glendalough by Markus Losack, offers study pilgrimages which 'have a contemplative and spiritual intent, drawing on the wealth of the Celtic tradition for our own spiritual formation and deepening'.[19] Recent destinations have included Jerusalem and Sinai as well as Irish sites, Iona, Lindisfarne and Durham and quiet days at Glendalough to tie in with saints' days and pre-Christian festivals. Since 1992 Cintra

Pemberton, a nun in the Episcopal Church of the USA, has run Celtic pilgrimages bringing Americans to Ireland, Wales and Scotland to visit the major early Christian sites. They combine the characteristic features of modern high-class holiday packages, en suite hotel rooms and luxury coach travel, with lectures on theology and church history, and regular morning and evening acts of worship. There are usually prayers at each of the sites visited and parts of each day are spent in silence. A particular feature of the programme is the Bendithion, a regular sharing of blessings and corporate thanksgiving rooted in the Welsh tradition of benediction.

In most respects these and other similar modern programmes seem closer to the later medieval than to the Celtic understanding of pilgrimage. They cater to a growing market for 'spiritual tourism' which is focused more on visiting particular places to gain a spiritual high than on cultivating a lifelong spirit of exile and finding one's desert place of resurrection. Yet we should not perhaps be too censorious about this mushrooming new branch of the package tourist industry. They are, after all, blurring the lines between tourism and pilgrimage and encouraging those who may be initially attracted by the lure of the holy place and the romantic destination to think about their own lives and the inner journey which was at the heart of the Celtic understanding of pilgrimage. If, as has been said, the distinction between tourists and pilgrims is that the former bring back gifts and the latter blessings, then perhaps we are seeing the emergence of a new category of pilgrim-tourists who return from their Celtic travels enriched by the Bendithion as well as laden with Highland knitwear and Waterford crystal.

In few places is the gap between tourism and pilgrimage being bridged more imaginatively or on such a massive scale as on the tiny island of Iona, now attracting over 250,000 day visitors a year. At one level Iona is a highly successful tourist attraction. There are often more than twenty tour buses parked at the ferry terminal at Fionnphort on Mull on an August day. For some of those they disgorge, the few hours spent on Columba's island may not differ from a visit to any other ancient monument or historic site – a walk round the abbey and its associated ruins to find the best angles for photos and a trip to the shop to buy a souvenir in the form of a Columba fridge magnet or a Wild Goose brooch. Yet most visitors can hardly be left unaware of the Iona Community's presence and its lively Christian witness and concern for contemporary issues. Those going into the Abbey are quite likely to find it adorned with banners and posters drawing attention to some campaign for peace and justice and to be asked if they would like to sign a petition to support prisoners of conscience or ban landmines. It is impossible to eat or drink at the café opposite the Abbey without being made aware of the issues of fair trade and environmental sustainability.

For those who stay on the island there is the opportunity to participate in the daily morning and evening services in the Abbey, with its exceptionally creative contemporary reworking of Celtic monastic patterns of worship, and to take part in seminars and workshops on a wide range of spiritual and ethical subjects. Every Wednesday between March and October visitors can join those staying in the Abbey and the MacLeod Centre on the Community's pilgrimage round the island which starts at 10.15 at the foot of St Martin's Cross in front of the abbey and ends around 4 p.m. in St Oran's Chapel, the oldest building on Iona, which stands in the nearby graveyard. Pilgrims walk across the island, sometimes in silence, pausing at places of particular significance for a time of meditation and prayer. In the ruins of the Augustinian nunnery there is a reflection on the neglect of women in history and their subordination through so many centuries by the Church. A stop at Loch Staonaig, a freshwater pool which for many years provided the island's water supply, provides the opportunity for a meditation on the significance of water in the Bible and its vital importance to so many communities today. At the bay where Columba is traditionally thought to have landed with his companions from Ireland pilgrims are encouraged to pick up two pebbles. One is thrown into the sea as a symbol of something in their lives they would like to leave behind, while the other is taken back as a sign of a new commitment. The whole day is, in the words of Peter Millar, a former warden of the Abbey and author of the *Pilgrim Guide to Iona*, 'a wonderful opportunity to reflect on the journey of your life, and the life of God's world'.[20]

Iona has become the best-known and most visited destination for contemporary Celtic pilgrims. Many find it a colony of heaven, or, in George MacLeod's famous phrase, 'a thin place', in which the boundaries between this world and the next are peculiarly blurred. It is a place where people find healing and new direction and where those brought together for the briefest encounters share their stories with significant results. This aspect is well captured in this poem written by Peter Millar towards the end of his time as warden of the abbey:

At Columba's Bay
they met;
Two of Iona's
countless pilgrims.
He, a pastor from Zaire;
She, a broker in Detroit.
And battered by the
autumn wind and rain
they shared their stories –
rooted in twentieth century realities,
yet both embedded
in a strange, life-giving
brokenness.
The hidden stories –

of poverty and torture,
of cancer and loneliness;
interweaving stories,
mirroring our
global interconnectedness.
And stories of faith;
of God's unfolding
in their lives
through ordinary days.
And suddenly it seemed
that for a moment
on that distant shore
they glimpsed
that basic truth –
that truly,
we are one
in Christ.[21]

Other Celtic sites around the British Isles have become meccas for the growing numbers of pilgrim-tourists. In my book, *Celtic Christianity: Making Myths and Chasing Dreams*, I suggest that Lindisfarne has come to occupy the role of symbolic heart of the current Celtic Christian revival that Iona did in the last revival, which took place in the late nineteenth and early twentieth century. This is partly a reflection of the well-deserved popularity of David Adam's prayers and the writings and activities of Ray Simpson and the Community of Aidan and Hilda and the Northumbria Community. It also reflects the strongly English and Anglican emphasis in the current revival, and the enthusiastic espousal of Celtic Christianity by charismatics and evangelicals as well as catholics and liberals. Other quieter and remoter Celtic sites like Pennant Melangell are also attracting ever more visitors. Part of their appeal undoubtedly lies in the fact that there is an element of adventure involved in reaching them, whether it is the long journey from Oban to Iona with two ferry crossings and the lengthy traverse of Mull, the excitement of crossing the causeway to Lindisfarne knowing that in a few hours it will be covered by the incoming tide, or the circuitous narrow road that leads up to Pennant Melangell. Yet remote as they are, these places are all essentially tourist destinations, easily accessible by car or coach. You don't have to get your feet wet or tramp across moorland and mountain to reach them.

Physically more demanding forms of pilgrimage, more akin to those with which the early Irish monks would have been familiar, are also proving increasingly popular. They chime in with the contemporary passion for outdoor pursuits and exercise and also with a rediscovery of the spiritual benefits of walking together. This dimension of pilgrimage has always been strong in the Irish Christian tradition and is perhaps most strongly demonstrated in the popularity of the climb up Croagh Patrick, the 2,500-feet-high mountain in the north-west of County Mayo, known locally as The Reek, on which

St Patrick is said to have fasted for forty days. The Reek has long been regarded as a holy mountain and was almost certainly a focus in pre-Christian times for celebrations of the Celtic god Lugh. Its lower slopes are dotted with the remains of prehistoric cromlechs, burial chambers, cup and ring markings and standing stones. It was first associated with Patrick in the life of the saint written by Tirechan in the late seventh century. By the ninth century it had become a major destination for penitential pilgrims. During the centuries of penal laws against Roman Catholicism in Ireland, the pilgrimages became a defiant focus of both Catholic and Irish sentiment. Attempts by local bishops to suppress the pilgrimages up the mountain in the latter part of the nineteenth century met fierce resistance, and the Reek has continued to maintain a key position in popular Irish spirituality, attracting significantly more pilgrims in recent years.

The largest and most significant pilgrimage up Croagh Patrick takes place on the last Sunday in July, known as Reek Sunday, when as many as 25,000 make their way up its steep slopes. I was deeply privileged to make the ascent on Reek Sunday 1999 in the company of an international group of pilgrims assembled by Tommy Murphy, a Columban missionary priest who has spent much of his life in China. The group, which included two Filipinos, three Koreans, a Fijian and a French enthusiast for Celtic mythology, had started their five day-pilgrimage at

Knock and slept on the bare boards of village halls along the way. I was only able to join them for the last leg of the walk after the much softer preparation of a comfortable night's bed and breakfast. It was still a marvellously moving and exhilarating experience. Equipped with the stout sticks which every pilgrim carries, we were set on our way early on the Sunday morning by a long extempore Celtic blessing-cum-journey prayer from a Holy Ghost father, which mingled pagan and Christian imagery around the 'deep peace' theme. Unlike most modern pilgrims who take the most direct way up, we followed the six-mile Tochar Phadraig (Patrick's Causeway), the old pilgrim route from Ballintuber Abbey which was reopened and waymarked in 1989 by the local parish priest.

As we walked on, sharing folk songs of our various lands and conversations about our own life journeys and experiences, the great conical mass of the Reek loomed ever closer with a broad black ribbon of what looked like ants crawling slowly up its scree-laden summit. The first two thousand or so feet of the ascent is a reasonably gentle climb up well-defined paths over turf and heather. The last five hundred feet involves scrambling up a pile of constantly shifting loose scree and stones which seems almost vertical in places. On this stage you are almost carried up by others, both physically by the sheer press of bodies gradually making their way up and spiritually by the constant encouragement of fellow climbers and those coming down from the top. At various points on the way up there are stations at which many of the pilgrims pause to recite a specified number of Hail Marys and Our Fathers. At the top there are other traditional penitential exercises to perform: walking seven times round *Leaba Phadraig* (Patrick's bed), a concrete slab surrounded by a tubular railing, kneeling at another shrine and walking fifteen times in a clockwise direction round the church built on the summit in 1904. Mass is celebrated at half-hourly intervals from early morning until late afternoon by priests stationed in a little glass-covered booth at the front of the church. On one side of the booth a door marked 'Confessions' leads to a room manned by a rota of priests, with at least six on duty at any one time, and on the other a door marked 'Communion' is opened at the end of each Mass for people to file through and receive the consecrated wafer.

One thing saddened me about the Croagh Patrick pilgrimage. On the summit a group of young people were handing out little green leaflets entitled *Croagh Patrick – a Place of Hope for the Irish*. Thinking that they must be about the history and spirit of the pilgrimage, I asked for one and was immediately treated to a fundamentalist Protestant attack on the whole spirit of the event. A girl from Northern Ireland attending a Bible college in England asked me if I did not find it sad that all these people felt by making this arduous climb and going through certain exercises they were somehow getting nearer to God. On the contrary, I retorted. As a Protestant minister, I found the whole pilgrimage deeply moving and only wished that it could be an ecumenical venture. I had no sense, as the protesters suggested, of a doctrine of salvation by works or idolatry towards Patrick. The eucharistic celebrations, which were in every sense the summit of the pilgrimage, were focused clearly on the person and work of Christ. All the way down the mountain, groups of Protestant protesters handed out further leaflets and also made their point by rearranging stones on the bare hills to spell out the message 'Salvation only through Jesus'. It was a sad reminder how Celtic Christianity, which has such potential to unite Ireland, can also be so divisive.

The central argument of the protesters' leaflet was that while those climbing Croagh Patrick were essentially hoping for something in the way of forgiveness and salvation, those who had come to Christ and accepted him as their personal saviour had the assurance of salvation through the substitutionary death of Christ. They were no longer hoping – they knew that they were going to heaven.[22] I was reminded of the distinction that I made in my book, *Marching to the Promised Land*, between two kinds of Christians that I labelled pilgrims and marchers:

The pilgrims continue on their quest, welcoming others as companions in a journey that has

many twists and deviations. The marchers have
a much clearer sense of their destination and a
greater certainty that they have already reached
it. They also believe that there is only one route
and feel an overwhelming compulsion to bring
others along it.'[23]

The experience of climbing Croagh Patrick under-
lined several aspects of pilgrimage which seem to me
to be highly relevant to the contemporary Christian
situation. The first is the simple pleasure of walking
together. I am pretty sure that I will never again in
this life see most of my companions on that walk. Yet
in the course of that Reek Sunday I developed a close
bond with them, all the more so because of that
painful slog up the mountain and the exhilaration of
reaching the top. They were all Catholics. I am a
Protestant. Most of them were non-British. I was
reminded of that inspired slogan, 'Not strangers but
pilgrims', used for the three-year interdenominational process of prayer, reflection and debate on the
nature and purpose of the Church which began in
1986 and brought well over half a million Christians
from many different church traditions together in
Lenten study groups. It was in direct response to the
great grass-roots pressure for ecumenism that came
out of this process that the leaders of the mainline
churches in Britain met at Swanwick in 1987 and
agreed a statement declaring that 'our Churches must
now move from co-operation to clear commitment

to each other, in search of the unity for which Christ prayed, and in common evangelism and service of the world'.[24]

How far this high aim is, in fact, being realised is debatable. What is clear, however, is that pilgrimage together, both literally and metaphorically, is proving one of the most meaningful ways in which Christians of different denominations break through the barriers which divide them and draw closer to each other. Perhaps pilgrimage may provide the model for ecumenical, and indeed inter-faith, dialogue, co-operation and commitment in the twenty-first century. The twentieth century was dominated by a more institutional and static concept of ecumenism based on worthy but unrealistic hopes of ecclesial union and agreements around bland doctrinal statements produced after fudging and mudging to find the lowest common denominator. The future for ecumenism perhaps rests much more with pilgrims setting out together, and concerned as much about their journey as their destination. Perhaps I may be permitted to quote again from *Marching to the Promised Land*:

> The ecumaniacs, those who felt the passionately held and long fought for differences between the churches could be ended by committees meeting and producing reports couched in sufficiently bland and vague terms, have had their day. In their place are genuine

pilgrims who recognize that the journey they
are making will involve pain and sacrifice, but
who feel it is worth while to tread the road
together, sharing, learning and maybe even
resting on one another's shoulders for a while,
but accepting too that in the end each may
diverge to take their own route to the promised land.[25]

A second theme which the Croagh Patrick climb
highlighted for me is the physicality of pilgrimage.
It takes us back to the manliness and muscular
nature of Celtic Christianity noted by Ray Simpson.
This is not a sexist or gender-specific matter.
Women are in many ways far more physical than
men. It was noticeable that far more women than
men followed the traditional penitential practice of
climbing barefoot up the Reek. The revival of
pilgrimage is part of a wider and welcome movement to put physicality back into faith by walking it
as well as talking it. There is, indeed, a whole theology and spirituality of walking to be explored and
rediscovered in terms of its essential rhythm and
naturalness. In the hundreds of thousands of years
of human evolution it is only in the last century that
most of us have travelled at more than four miles
an hour. There is also an important pastoral dimension to walking together. I know of several ministers
who reckon that some of their most significant
pastoral work is undertaken on long hill walks

with those who are feeling guilty, weary and heavy laden.

The physicality of pilgrimage has another important contemporary message. It reminds us that there are other ways of praying apart from sitting with a book or kneeling in a church. The features of the island landscape on Iona and the stations on Croagh Patrick provide physical and visual prompts for prayer and meditation. But we do not have to be on a Hebridean island or an Irish mountain to engage in physical prayer. One of the most intriguing recent developments in the field of Christian spirituality has been the rediscovery of the medieval practice of prayer walks and labyrinths. In the United States especially, Christians of several different denominations are making and using labyrinths in churches, backyards and even in their kitchens. These range from large and complex designs, painted or inlaid on to church floors which can be walked by several hundred people at any one time, to finger labyrinths in the form of Celtic spirals and interlacing made out of salt dough. Unlike mazes, labyrinths have only one path which ends up at the centre after numerous twists and turns and doubling back on itself. Several North American hospitals and psychotherapists are using labyrinths to encourage meditation and healing and labyrinth walks are springing up on university campuses. This is just one dimension of a reawakening to the spiritual benefits of prayer that is walked rather than just talked. In his book *Stations* Simon

Bailey suggested ways of praying at different places in one's own home.[26] We still have some way to go before emulating the full physical rigours of early Celtic prayer – I have yet to meet anyone who wades waist deep into the sea to recite the psalms or spends long hours genuflecting or with arms stretched out in the cross vigil – but we are at least begining to explore alternatives to sedentary and passive prayer and to realise that in this activity we don't have to be couch potatoes.

Pilgrimage, certainly when it is on the scale of the annual climb up Croagh Patrick, is very public as well as being very physical. It presents a clear and open witness to Christ and the enduring importance to many people of the gospel. Pilgrimages are very photogenic events which tend to be reported on in newspapers and television news programmes. When I reached the summit of Croagh Patrick I was interviewed by a journalist from Denmark and a documentary film crew, and three helicopters hired by television networks were circling overhead. The opportunity to make a very public witness to the Christian faith and to gain media coverage has undoubtedly been another factor in the recent upsurge of interest in pilgrimages and related events. The annual March for Jesus, which began in 1987 with a march through London organised by the Ichthus Fellowship, has brought a very visible Christian presence on to the streets of British towns and cities. It has also raised the profile of spiritual

warfare and redeeming the land from the forces of
Satan in a way that is highly reminiscent of the outlook and activities attributed to many of the Celtic
saints. For four weeks in the summer of 1997 'The
Walk of 1,000 Men', organised by Through Faith
Missions, involved over a thousand men and women
walking through Kent, preaching, meeting people,
anointing the sick and evangelising in pubs, schools,
street markets, railway stations and at street corners in
towns and villages across the country. Less overtly evangelistic, but displaying an equally public Christian
face, were the pilgrimages organised across the British
Isles in 1997 in connection with the 1400th anniversary of the death of Columba and the coming of
Augustine to Canterbury, and in 1999 to mark the
dawning of the third millennium. The starting points
for this latter event, entitled Pilgrimage 2000, which
involved pilgrims on seven routes converging on
Canterbury for an evening vigil on 31 December
1999, included significant Celtic Christian sites such
as Iona, Lindisfarne and St David's.

Those taking part in a pilgrimage are also able to
connect in a particularly vivid way with the
Communion of Saints. As I toiled up the final steep
slope of Croagh Patrick, I was very conscious of the
hundreds of thousands who had climbed up before
me over the centuries and whose feet had gradually
worn the outline of a track over the loose shale and
stones. Pilgrimage links us in an almost tangible way
with the great ongoing Christian story as we walk

literally in the footsteps of those who have gone
before us in the faith. It reminds us of our spiritual
roots and traditions, while at the same time
pointing us onwards and forwards. As one of my
students put it, pilgrimage involves looking back in
order to look forward. Cintra Pemberton observes
that 'the Communion of Saints takes on a new and
profound meaning when visiting holy places long
associated with holy people'.[27] She rightly points
out that this communion embraces not just the
long dead saints associated with particular churches
or shrines but also the countless thousands who have
come there as pilgrims through the ages and those
who care for the sites today. In her book, Soulfaring, she
quotes lines from T. S. Eliot's 'Little Gidding', one of
the Four Quartets, which speak eloquently of this aspect
of pilgrimage to holy places:

> If you came this way,
> Taking any route, starting from anywhere,
> At any time or at any season,
> It would always be the same: you would have
>   to put off
> Sense and notion. You are not here to verify,
> Instruct yourself, or inform curiosity
> Or carry report. You are here to kneel
> Where prayer has been valid. And prayer is
>   more
> Than an order of words, the conscious
>   occupation

Of the praying mind, or the sound of the voice
   praying.
And what the dead had no speech for, when
   living,
They can tell you, being dead: the
   communication
Of the dead is tongued with fire beyond the
   language of the living.[28]

In Celtic Christianity, as we have seen, pilgrimage
was not just an outward, physical experience but
also symbolised an inner journey of perpetual exile
and seeking after Christ. This dimension is equally
important for us to recover today, and perhaps
rather more difficult and disturbing than the enjoy-
able business of striding out on a pilgrim walk
together. We tend to pick our destinations, unlike
the Irish monks who cast off from home and
security without any clear idea of where they were
going. Many of us, myself included, are not very
good at letting go, taking risks and plunging into the
unknown, trusting ourselves utterly to God. It is
significant that the idea of letting go is so prominent
in modern pastoral care and counselling, especially
in respect of those experiencing grief, bereavement
and life-changing situations.[29] It is well expressed in
another context in the experiences of a Methodist
youth pastor from South Africa who spent a year as a
pilgrim in Europe, working for his keep in each
place:

Lindisfarne was one of the most poignant steps
on my journey. Praying one day on St
Cuthbert's Island, I had the sense of truly being
in a coracle – that in truth I had actually
pushed away from the shore of my life, and
was now upon the vast sea with God. It was a
momentous discovery for me because I had
been in the mindset of wondering when, if
ever, I would have had enough courage to push
away from the shore. Meantime my very act of
pilgrimage had already thrust me out onto
waters, and my life will never be the same
again.[30]

Taking risks, letting go, casting off, trusting to
God – all these are suggested by the metaphor of
pilgrimage. Other elements are identified in an
article by Elizabeth McClean in a recent issue of the
Iona Community's magazine *The Coracle* devoted to the
theme of the 'Pilgrim Way':

Stepping lightly, tripping, turning, finding the
signs are gone, the experience of having only
the horizon before me. This is my pilgrimage.
This is the journey I am called to make, without sense nor in the hope of any destinatiuon
but the ground on which I tread as I go.[31]

Perhaps one of the most important messages that the
Celtic Christian emphasis on pilgrimage gives us
today is to return to the ancient notion of Christians

as the people of (and on) the Way. This does not have to be the Celtic way but it does involve a self-understanding of Christians as travellers and voyagers and a view of the Church as an essentially provisional community. A pilgrim church lives lightly to buildings, financial support and hierarchies. Too many churches today, feeling beleaguered and threatened, have abandoned pilgrimage and provisionality for an outlook and structure more appropriate to narrow sectarianism. There is much wisdom in Jean Vanier's observation that 'a sect has control at its heart, a community has journey at its heart'.[32]

In recovering the idea of the pilgrim Church, we return to one of the fundamental themes in the Old Testament. A good number of the psalms which were so well loved and influential in Celtic Christianity were clearly written to be sung on pilgrimages to Jerusalem, and make much use of the motifs of walking and journeying. It is of course true that in the monarchic period, God was worshipped and indeed seen as having his earthly dwelling in a very specific place, the temple in Jerusalem. Yet the earlier Israelite tradition that God could not be pinned down and limited to one particular place was never abandoned and was regularly invoked by the prophets. When David first proposed building a permanent temple, the Lord told him through Nathan, 'I have not dwelt in a house since the day I brought up the people of Israel from Egypt to this day, but I have been moving about in a tent for my dwelling' (2 Samuel 7:6 RSV).

Much earlier, God had revealed himself to Moses as the God of the Exodus, constantly moving with and ahead of his people.

This sense of the pilgrim God, who has no fixed abode on earth but travels with his people and is perhaps closest to them in the experience of wandering through the wilderness, is echoed in Jesus' well-known words recorded in Matthew 8:20 (RSV): 'Foxes have holes, and birds of the air have nests; but the Son of man has nowhere to lay his head.' It has profound implications for ecclesiology, suggesting that the Church should see itself more as a community or movement than as an institution or fixed establishment.

Another Old Testament theme we would do well to recover is the connection between pilgrimage and sabbath. In ancient Israel, as in Irish monasteries, pilgrimage brought people out of their everyday routine and gave their lives rhythm and balance. There is a deep need in our increasingly stressed out and frenetic society to affirm the importance of 'holy rest', quiet days (and weeks), retreats and sabbaticals. For a long time only university academics have been given paid sabbaticals. The principle is slowly being extended to clergy. It should be extended also to doctors, nurses, social workers, train drivers, shop assistants, factory production-line workers, indeed to all those whose normal work leaves them drained and stressed and who need the spiritual and other benefits of periods of pilgrimage away from the routine and pressure of their everyday jobs.

There is something marvellously counter-cultural about the whole principle of pilgrimage in a society such as ours which puts such a high premium on material success, output and added value. After ten years of studying and living with Celtic Christianity, I remain unsure whether it exemplifies Richard Niebuhr's 'Christ against culture' or 'Christ of culture.' There is evidence both ways. The Celtic saints are often portrayed as directly confronting pagan practitioners and waging spiritual warfare. Yet they also baptised and blessed pre-Christian traditions and holy places. Pilgrimage itself may well have been a culture-friendly concept among the naturally wandering Celtic peoples of the sixth and seventh centuries. Perhaps today it also resonates with a post-modern culture where there is much fluidity and movement. Yet there is also something very counter-cultural about extolling the value of pilgrimage today, a point well brought out in the editorial in the recent issue of *Coracle* from which I have already quoted:

> Pilgrimage is a sign of contradiction, and of
> resistance to our prevailing value system, that
> of the market. Pilgrimage, after all, has no
> function other than itself; its means is as
> important as its end, its process as its product.
> Its utility value is small, and its benefits cannot
> be quantified or costed. Its value is intrinsic. It

is something that is good to do because it is good to do. It states clearly that the extravagant gesture (because it is extravagant in terms of time and commitment) is an irrepressible part of what it means to be human and to walk on the earth. And whether the context for pilgrimage is solitude or community, we will draw deeper into the mystery of God and the care of creation.[33]

There is another important way in which the concept of pilgrimage is particularly relevant today. It is the way in which more and more people seem to be coming to Christian faith. A survey of 500 adult Christians spread across the denominations in 1991 revealed that for most coming to faith was a gradual process rather than a sudden conversion. While 31 per cent of respondents spoke of a particular moment of decision or conversion which could be dated exactly, 69 per cent spoke rather of a journey to faith lasting for a considerable period of time. In some cases this journey took up to forty or more years, although the average time was around four years. This finding was in marked contrast to the results of a survey undertaken in 1967 when the proportions of those experiencing a sudden conversion and a gradual journey to faith were exactly reversed. It suggests that far more people are now pilgrims, coming to faith through a gradual process rather than a sudden crisis. A report compiled on the basis of the 1991 survey by John Finney in his role as the Church of England's officer for the Decade of Evangelism recommended that churches should focus less on 'sudden conversion' methods of evangelism which look for quick results and more on strategies to enable people towards a gradual discovery of God. Among these strategies it specifically commended friendship evangelism and mentoring.[34] John Finney has subsequently argued in his book *Recovering the Past* that the Celtic Christian approach to mission with its model of gradual inculturation is much more appropriate to evangelising modern Britain than the Roman way of building and imposing institutional structures. He sees the latter approach as exemplifying the paradigm of Paul's sudden conversion on the road to Damascus, whereas the Celtic way echoes the experience of the two disciples on the road to Emmaus, their faith gradually opened up by the stranger who walks with them along the road.[35]

The pilgrim model is relevant in other ways to the state of post-modern Christianity. An increasing number of Christians are travelling during the course of their journey of faith from one church and denomination to another. It is less and less common for individuals to spend their entire lives worshipping in the same building as so many of our ancestors did. This is only partly because of much greater social and geographical mobility. It is also because of cultural and social influences. One of my St Andrews students, asked for a contemporary definition of pilgrimage, replied 'not spending your whole Christian life in one church'. Church-hopping, like channel-hopping, is a feature of our contemporary pick-and-mix, choice-driven culture. Statistics clearly show that among those who attend church today there is much less 'brand loyalty' to a particular place or denomination and that even regular worshippers often move through a cycle of dipping in and out of widely different types of church. There is clearly a negative side to this trend – it betokens a lack of commitment and a consumerist mentality that encourages people to flit around and move on to a new church as soon as they tire of their old one. It also presents serious financial problems for churches who have traditionally depended on regular covenanted giving from long-term committed members. Yet this kind of pilgrimage is also potentially very liberating and enriching. It prevents people getting stuck in a rut and seeing churchgoing as a routine duty. It encourages variety, growth and new insights and challenges along the faith journey.

Pilgrimage is ultimately about hope. To that extent the protesters giving out the leaflet entitled *Croagh Patrick – a Place of Hope for the Irish* were absolutely right. Hope is one of the great Christian virtues, perhaps the most neglected in Paul's famous trio of faith, hope and charity. It has been well said that the opposite of Christian faith is not so much doubt as certainty. In a similar way, the opposite of Christian hope is not so much despair as easy, complacent optimism. Christian hope is grounded in the cross of Christ, that cross which, in the words of the great Scottish hymn-writer George Matheson, 'lifteth up my head'. Its essential quality is its 'not yetness', so well delineated in our age by Jürgen Moltmann. It looks beyond the here and now, beyond the crucifixion-resurrection continuum, to the ultimate completion and fulfilment promised in the *eschaton* when all will be gathered up in Christ.

I am increasingly persuaded that in all my writings on Celtic Christianity I have not made nearly enough of its eschatological dimension. A recent thesis by James Bruce argues very convincingly that the miracle stories in Adamnan's *Life of Columba* are there essentially to bring an eschatological perspective, as signs of the breaking in of the Kingdom of God and pointers to the coming 'last things' of judgement and consummation.[36] I suspect the same may be true of many other texts that have come down to us from Celtic Christianity's golden age. It is certainly the case with Columba's own *Altus Prosator*, which, as we have seen, is filled with the eschatological themes of Christ's coming again in glory and judgement. We are brought back to the notion of colonies of heaven that has provided the theme for this book. Christians inhabit the in-between times, living in a perpetual Advent state, waiting and hoping for the glory of God to be revealed. Unfulfilled as this condition of 'not yetness' may be, it is also suffused with those glimpses of glory that we do already have in our sacramental world so thinly divided from the world to come. Together with the great promises of God, they give us the grounds, in the words of Charles Wesley's great hymn, 'to rejoice in glorious hope', to celebrate and explore the heavenly in the earthly and the spiritual in the physical, by creating colonies of heaven on earth.

Pilgrimage, in the Celtic rather than the medieval or modern understanding, is at least as much about travelling hopefully as about arriving. Modern churches are often obsessed with arriving at destinations, whether it be attendance figures, achieving conversions, meeting quotas or fulfilling targets set in mission audits and action plans. In the Christian life, we arrive only to depart again. We climb the mountain and then descend it. We are in a constant state of *metanoia*, conversion and change. We are always travelling, often on circuitous detours and sometimes backwards rather than forwards, sustained by the glimpses we are given on the way of the glories that are revealed of what is to come and what breaks through the veil.

Pilgrims are perhaps above all else seekers. They are on that journey of exploration whose object is so beautifully encapsulated in the familiar words of Richard of Chichester's prayer, 'O most merciful redeemer, friend and brother, may we know thee more clearly, love thee more dearly and follow thee more nearly.' I find it profoundly symbolic and significant that, according to Adamnan, the last

words from the Bible copied out by Columba in his
earthly life came from Psalm 34: 'Those that seek the
Lord shall not want for anything that is good.' It is
not those who have found the Lord, who have
reached their destination and feel they know all the
answers, that the psalmist addressed here, but rather
those who are still searching and on a journey. I find
myself coming back to the image of the Celtic knot
with which I began my first book on Celtic
Christianity and which I proposed as a metaphor for
our spiritual journeys, meandering, confused and
often doubling back on themselves, yet always cir-
cumscribed and encompassed by God's providential
love and care. I also find myself wanting to end this
book, as I have all my previous ones on Celtic
Christianity, with a poem. Julie McGuinness'
'Reflections on Life's Road' captures the pilgrim
spirit of Celtic Christianity, so helpful and hopeful for
us as we enter the third millennium:

> Some people travel in straight lines:
> Sat in metal boxes, eyes ahead,
> Always mindful of their target,
> Moving in obedience to coloured lights and
>   white lines,
> Mission accomplished at journey's end.
>
> Some people travel round in circles:
> Trudging in drudgery, eyes looking down,
> Knowing only too well their daily, unchanging
>   round,

Moving in response to clock and to habit,
Journey never finished yet never begun.

I want to travel in patterns of God's making:
Walking in wonder, gazing all around,
Knowing my destiny, though not my
   destination,
Moving to the rhythm of the surging of his
   spirit,
A journey which when life ends, in Christ has
   just begun.[37]

Notes

Except where otherwise stated, the place of publication of books mentioned is London.

Preface

1 G. MacLeod, 'Man is made to rise' in *The Whole Earth Shall Cry Glory* (Wild Goose Publications, Glasgow, 1985), p. 16.
2 I. Bradley, *Celtic Christianity: Making Myths and Dreaming Dreams* (Edinburgh University Press, Edinburgh, 1999), p. vii.
3 Ibid., p. ix.

Chapter 1: Colonies of Heaven – the Monastic Model

1 M. Herren, 'Mission and monasticism in the *Confessio* of Patrick', in D. O Corráin (ed.), *Sages, Saints and Storytellers: Celtic Studies in Honour of Professor James Carney* (An Sagart, Maynooth, 1989), pp. 76–85.
2 W. Davies, *Wales in the Early Middle Ages* (Leicester University Press, Leicester, 1982), p. 141.
3 Ibid., p. 146.
4 K. Hughes, *The Church in Early Irish Society* (Methuen, 1966).

5 R. Sharpe, 'Churches and communities in early medieval Ireland: towards a pastoral model' in J. Blair and R. Sharpe (eds), *Pastoral Care before the Parish* (Leicester University Press, Leicester, 1992), p. 84.

6 Davies, *Wales in the Early Middle Ages*, p. 149.

7 A. Thacker, 'Monks, preaching and pastoral care in early Anglo-Saxon England' in Blair and Sharpe, *Pastoral Care*, p. 139.

8 Bede, *Life of Cuthbert* 7.

9 Adamnan, *Life of Columba* I, 48.

10 Bede, *Ecclesiastical History* IV, 26.

11 Blair and Sharpe, *Pastoral Care*, p. 7.

12 The Rule of Columcille as printed in the appendix of S. Stone, *Lays of Iona and Other Poems* (Longmans, Green & Co., 1897), p. 112.

13 P. Sheldrake, *Living Between Worlds: Place and Journey in Celtic Spirituality* (Darton, Longman & Todd, 1995), p. 39.

14 C. Rowland, 'Friends of Albion?' in S. Platten and C. Lewis (eds), *Flagships of the Spirit* (Darton, Longman & Todd, 1998), p. 32.

15 N. Alldrit, 'Cathedrals and their communities' in Platten and Lewis, *Flagships of the Spirit*, p. 49.

16 Platten and Lewis, 'Setting a course' in *Flagships of the Spirit*, p. 179.

17 R. van de Weyer, *Celtic Gifts* (Canterbury Press, Norwich, 1997).

18 *Church Times* (3 May 1996), p. 5.

19 *Church Times*, 13 February 1998.

20 *The Times*, 3 December 1997.

21 V. Hugo, *Les Misérables* (Everyman's Library, 1998), p. 506.

22 Ibid., pp. 507, 509.

23 T. Merton, *Conjectures of a Guilty Bystander* (Image Books, New York, 1968), p. 177.

24 V. Hugo, *Les Misérables*, p. 518.

25 Ibid., pp. 518–19.

26 Community of Aidan and Hilda: Handbook for Explorers and Members (unpublished, 1st edn, 1999), Chapter 2.

27 *Church Times*, 30 July 1999.

28 N. Shanks, *Iona – God's Energy* (Hodder & Stoughton, 1999).

29 I. Smith, 'Commitment counts', *Life and Work* (February 1999), p. 25.

Chapter 2: **Blessing and Cursing**

1 E. Bowen, *Priest-Poet* (Church in Wales Publications, Cardiff, 1993), pp. 142–7. On the Welsh praise poem tradition, see A. M. Allchin, *Praise Above All* (University of Wales Press, Cardiff, 1991), O. Davies, *Celtic Christianity in Early Medieval Wales* (University of Wales Press, Cardiff, 1996) and B. O'Malley, *A Welsh Pilgrim's Manual* (Gomer, Llandysul, 1989).

2 Adamnan, *Vita Columbae* II, 26.

3 R. Loomis and D. Johnston (eds), *Medieval Welsh Poems: An Anthology*, Medieval and Renaissance Texts and Studies, No. 86 (Binghamton, New York, 1992). I owe this reference to Donald Allchin.

4 Adamnan, *Vita Columbae* II, 6.

5 Translation of St Patrick's Breastplate by Noel O'Donoghue in J. Mackey (ed.), *Introduction to Celtic Christianity* (T. & T. Clark, Edinburgh, 1989), p. 48.

6 A. Carmichael, *Carmina Gadelica* (Floris Books, Edinburgh, 1992), p. 222.

7 Adamnan, *Vita Columbae* II, 16.

8 Ibid., II, 29.

9 Quoted by D. Allchin, 'The world as sacrament: perspectives from Iona on the solidarity of all things in Christ', *Essex Papers in Theology and Society*, No. 17 (1999), pp. 28–9.

10 J. Macquarrie, *Paths in Spirituality* (SCM Press, 1989), pp. 122–3.

11 I. Bradley, *The Celtic Way* (Darton, Longman & Todd, 1993), p. 101; G. MacLeod, *The Whole Earth Shall Cry Glory* (Wild Goose Publications, Glasgow, 1985), pp. 13, 16.

12 Carmichael, *Carmina Gadelica*, p. 45.

13 O. Davies and F. Bowie, *Celtic Christian Spirituality* (SPCK, 1995), p. 54.

14 Davies, *Celtic Christianity in Early Medieval Wales*, p. 86.

15 Allchin, *Praise Above All*, p. 6.

16 Adamnan, *Vita Columbae* II, 25.

17 Bede, *Ecclesiastical History* III, 5.

18 Psalm 109: 17 and Psalm 137: 8–9 (REB).

19 This is based on a lecture given by John Bell to my pastoral care and counselling class at St Andrews in April 1999.

20 I owe these thoughts, and comments, to an article by Ian Cowie, minister of Kinross, 'How meaningful is the blessing?' in the Church of Scotland's *Ministers' Forum* for June 1999.

21 R. Simpson, *Celtic Blessings for Everday Life* (Hodder, 1998).

22 E. Sitwell, 'Praise We Great Men' in *The Outcasts* (Macmillan, 1962).

Chapter 3: Penance and Pastoral Care

1 J. Blair and R. Sharpe (eds), *Pastoral Care before the Parish* (Leicester University Press, Leicester, 1992), p. 74.

2 J. T. McNeill, *A History of the Cure of Souls* (SCM Press, 1951), Ch. VII.

3 H. Connolly, *The Irish Penitentials* (Four Courts Press, Dublin, 1995), p. 1.

4 Ibid., p.15.

5 L. Bieler, *The Irish Penitentials* (Dublin Institute for Advanced Studies, Dublin, 1963), p. 85.

6 Quoted in L. Byrne (ed.), *Traditions of Spiritual Guidance* (Geoffrey Chapman, 1990), p. 34.

7 B. Ward, *The Lives of the Desert Fathers* (Cistercian Publications, Kalamazoo, Michigan & Mowbray, Oxford, 1981), p. 13.

8 Connolly, *The Irish Penitentials*, pp. 201–2.

9 Ibid., p. 154.

10 Ibid., p. 11.

11 McNeill, *Cure of Souls*, p. 127.

12 Adamnan, *Vita Columbae* II, 41.

13 Ibid., II, 39.

14 Bieler, *The Irish Penitentials*, p. 103.

15 E. Sutherland, *Ravens and Black Rain: The Story of Highland Second Sight* (Constable, 1985).

16 On this see Gilbert Markus' unpublished paper on 'The Book of Deer and the Visitation of the Sick' given at the day conference

Notes

on the Book of Deer organised by the Elphinstone Institute and held in the University of Aberdeen in September 1997.

17 W. Stokes (ed.), *The Martyrology of Oengus the Culdee* (Henry Bradshaw Society, 1905), p. 465.

18 Connolly, *The Irish Penitentials*, p. 208, n. 50.

19 L.Byrne (ed.), *Traditions of Spiritual Guidance*, p. 34.

20 R. Simpson, *Soul-Friendship: Celtic Insights into Spiritual Mentoring* (Hodder & Stoughton, 1999), p. 166.

21 Ibid.

22 M. Kennedy-Fraser and K. MacLeod, *Songs of the Hebrides* (Boosey & Co., 1909). Vol. I, p. 104.

23 Carmichael, *Carmina Gadelica* (Floris Books, Edinburgh, 1992), p. 578.

24 Ibid.

25 Connolly, *The Irish Penitentials*, p.16.

26 See, for example, Paul Goodliff's *Pastoral Care in a Confused Climate* (Darton, Longman & Todd, 1998), and Francis Bridger and David Atkinson's *Counselling in Context* (Darton, Longman & Todd, 1998).

27 Simpson, *Soul-Friendship*, p.4.

28 Quoted in A. Raine and J. Skinner (eds), *Celtic Daily Prayer: A Northumbrian Office* (Marshall Pickering, 1994), p. 358.

29 P. Wilcock, *The Spiritual Care of Dying and Bereaved People* (SPCK, 1996), p. 3.

30 Simpson, *Soul-Friendship*, p. 65.

31 A. Smith (ed.), *TM: An Aid to Christian Growth* (Mayhew McCrimmon, 1983).

32 Connolly, *The Irish Penitentials*, p. 136.

33 R. A. Lambourne, 'Counselling for Narcissus or counselling for Christ' in M. Wilson (ed.), *Explorations in Health and Salvation* (University of Birmingham Press, Birmingham, 1983). See also the books mentioned in note 26 above.

34 *Church Times* (12 November 1999), p. 6.

35 A. Campbell, *Rediscovering Pastoral Care* (Darton, Longman & Todd, 1986), H. Nouwen, *The Wounded Healer* (Darton, Longman & Todd, 1994), J. Vanier, *The Broken Body* (Darton, Longman & Todd, 1988).

36 Connolly, *The Irish Penitentials*, p. 178.

Chapter 4: Worship

1 A. Carmichael, *Carmina Gadelica* (Floris Books, Edinburgh, 1992), p. 30.

2 M. Herbert, *Iona, Kells and Derry* (Clarendon Press, Oxford, 1988), p. 264. On the use of the psalms in the early desert monastic communities see G. Woolfenden, 'The use of the Psalter by early monastic communities', *Studia Patristica* Vol. XXVI (1993), pp. 88–94.

3 Adamnan, *Vita Columbae* II, 9.

4 T. Clancy and G. Markus, *Iona: The Earliest Poetry of a Celtic Monastery* (Edinburgh University Press, Edinburgh, 1995), p. 111.

5 J. Purser, *Scotland's Music* (Mainstream, Edinburgh, 1992), pp. 39–45.

6 Clancy and Markus, *Iona*, p. 73.

7 G. Walker, *Sancti Columbani Opera* (Dublin Institute for Advanced Studies, Dublin, 1967), p. 65.

8 *Book of Common Order of the Church of Scotland* (St Andrew Press, Edinburgh, 1994), p. 523.

9 M. Perham, 'A plea for poetry and common prayer', *Church Times* (28 July 1995), p. 7.

10 *Church Times*, 14 May 1999.

11 A. Tilby, 'Risen, ascended, glorified', *Church Times* (14 May 1999), p. 13.

12 Clancy and Markus, *Iona*, p. 53.

Chapter 5: The Communion of Saints

1 D. Brown & T. Clancy (eds), *Spes Scotorum: Hope of Scots* (T. & T. Clark, Edinburgh, 1999), p. 3.

2 P. Brown, *The Cult of the Saints* (University of Chicago Press, Chicago, 1981), p. 3.

3 T. Head, *Hagiography and the Cult of the Saints: The Diocese of Orleans, 800–1200* (Cambridge University Press, Cambridge, 1990), p. 287.

4 Adamnan, *Vita Columbae* III, 8.

5 J. Blair and R. Sharpe (eds), *Pastoral Care before the Parish* (Leicester University Press, Leicester, 1992), pp. 69, 75.

6 P. O Riain, 'Towards a methodology in early Irish hagiography', *Peritia* Vol. I (1982), pp.146–59.

7 A. Carmichael, *Carmina Gadelica* (Floris Books, Edinburgh, 1992), p. 60.

8 Ibid., pp. 101, 105.

9 Ibid., p. 122.

10 A. M. Allchin and E. de Waal, *Threshold of Light* (Darton, Longman & Todd, 1986), p. 39. This translation of Gwenallt's Yr Eglwys was made by A. M. Hodge and is reproduced with the permission of A. M. Allchin.

11 A. M. Allchin, *God's Presence Makes the World* (Darton, Longman & Todd, 1997), p. 98.

12 Ibid., pp. 98–9. The translation is by A. M. Allchin and reproduced by permission.

13 See especially J. Richards, S. Wilson and L. Woodhead (eds) *Diana – the Making of a Media Saint* (I. B. Tauris, 1999) and A. Kear and D. L. Steinberg, *Mourning Diana – Nation, Culture and the Performance of Grief* (Routledge, 1999).

14 T. Harrison, *Diana – Icon and Sacrifice* (Lion Publishing, Oxford, 1998), pp. 162–3, 39–40.

15 Richards, Wilson and Woodhead, *Diana*, p. 3.

16 Quoted in *Sunday Telegraph* (11 July 1999), p. 9.

17 B. Hume, *Footprints of the Northern Saints* (Darton, Longman & Todd, 1996), p. 9.

18 *Daily Telegraph*, 30 November 1999.

19 *Tablet*, 26 June 1999.

20 *The Divine Life of the Church* (Scottish Church Society Conference and Series), Vol. II (Edinburgh, 1895), p. 38.

21 G. F. MacLeod, *The Whole Earth Shall Cry Glory* (Wild Goose Publications, Glasgow, 1985), p. 60.

Chapter 6: Pilgrimage

1 I. Bradley, *The Celtic Way* (Darton Longman & Todd, 1993), pp. 76–7.

2 S. Lawhead, *Byzantium* (HarperCollins, 1996), p. 19.

3 G. S. M. Walker (ed.), *Sancti Columbani Opera* (Institute for Advanced Studies, Dublin, 1957), p. 85.

4 L. Bieler (ed.), *The Irish Penitentials* (Institute for Advanced Studies, Dublin, 1963), p. 267.

5 Adamnan, *Vita Columbae* II, 42.

6 Ibid., I, 76.

7 *Sancti Columbani Opera*, p. 85.

8 R. Simpson, *Exploring Celtic Spirituality* (Hodder & Stoughton, 1995), p. 76.

9 T. O'Fiaich, *Columbanus in His Own Words* (Veritas, Dublin, 1974), p. 112.

10 P. Cavill, *Anglo-Saxon Christianity* (Fount, 1999), pp. 78–80.

11 J. Wooding, 'The *Navigatio Sancti Brendani Abbatis* and the world's end' (paper delivered to the Eleventh International Congress of Celtic Studies, Cork, 16 July 1999).

12 H. Connolly, *The Irish Penitentials* (Four Courts Press, Dublin, 1995), p. 177.

13 Ibid., p. 164.

14 Ibid., p. 79.

15 Ibid., p. 188.

16 Anonymous translation in *Church Hymnary* 3rd edn (Oxford University Press, Oxford, 1973), No. 398.

17 A. Carmichael, *Carmina Gadelica* (Floris Book, Edinburgh, 1992), p. 247.

18 The Sacred Land Project, press release 1997.

19 Celi De Ireland, programme leaflet 1997.

20 P. W. Millar, *Iona* (Canterbury Press, Norwich, 1997), p. 5.

21 P. W. Millar, 'Iona 1997', sent out with Christmas letter 1997. Quoted with permission.

22 D. Keogh, *Croagh Patrick – a Place of Hope for the Irish* (Cherith Gospel Outreach, Thurles, Co. Tipperary, 1998).

23 I. C. Bradley, *Marching to the Promised Land: Has the Church a Future?* (John Murray, 1992), p. 62.

24 Ibid., p. 46.

25 Ibid., pp. 47–8.

26 S. Bailey, *Stations* (Cairns Publications, Sheffield, 1991).

Notes

27 C. Pemberton, *Soulfaring: Celtic Pilgrimage Then and Now* (SPCK, 1999), p. 4.

28 T. S. Eliot, 'Little Gidding', lines 39–51 in *Four Quartets* (Faber & Faber, 1942).

29 See, for example, I. Ainsworth-Smith and P. Speck, *Letting Go: Caring for the Dying and Bereaved* (SPCK, 1982) and J. V. Taylor, *A Matter of Life and Death* (SCM Press, 1986), p. 67.

30 *The Aidan Way* No. 17 (February 1999), p. 9.

31 *Coracle* (April 1977), p. 11.

32 J. Vanier, *Community and Growth* (Darton, Longman & Todd, 1989), p. 1.

33 *Coracle* (April 1977), p. 4.

34 J. Finney, *Finding Faith Today* (Bible Society, 1992).

35 J. Finney, *Recovering the Past* (Darton, Longman & Todd, 1996), pp. 40–1.

36 J. Bruce, 'The nature and function of the marvellous in Adomnan's *Life of Columba*' (University of St Andrews PhD thesis, 1999).

37 J. McGuinness, 'Reflections of Life's Road', *The Aidan Way*, No. 12 (Samhain 1997).

Index

Index